TILL VICTORY IS WON

Black Soldiers in the Civil War

LIFT EV'RY VOICE AND SING

Lift ev'ry voice and sing,
Till earth and heaven ring,
Ring with the harmonies of liberty;
Let our rejoicing rise
High as the list'ning skies
Let it resound loud as the rolling sea.

Sing a song full of the faith that the dark past has
  taught us,
Sing a song full of the hope that the present has
  brought us;
Facing the rising sun of our new day begun,
Let us march on till victory is won.

(First two stanzas of a song inspired by the Emancipation Proclamation, written in 1900 by James Weldon Johnson and put to music by his brother, J. Rosamond Johnson. Adopted as the black national anthem.)

TILL VICTORY IS WON

Black Soldiers in the Civil War

Zak Mettger

LODESTAR BOOKS
Dutton   New York

for Esther

Library of Congress Cataloging-in-Publication Data

Mettger, Zak.
    Till victory is won: black soldiers in the Civil War / Zak Mettger. — 1st ed.
        p.   cm. — (Young readers' history of the Civil War)
    Includes bibliographical references and index.
    ISBN 0-525-67412-8
    1. United States—History—Civil War, 1861–1865—Participation, Afro-American—Juvenile literature.   2. Afro-American soldiers—History—19th century—Juvenile literature.   3. United States—History—Civil War, 1861–1965. [1. United States—History—Civil War, 1861–1865—Participation, Afro-American.   2. Afro-American soldiers.   3. United States—History—Civil War, 1861–1865.]   I. Title.   II. Series.
E540.N3M48   1994
973.7'415—dc20   93-44154
                                                                                   CIP
                                                                                    AC

Published in the United States by Lodestar Books,
an affiliate of Dutton Children's Books,
a division of Penguin Books USA Inc.
375 Hudson Street
New York, N.Y. 10014

Published simultaneously in Canada by
McClelland & Stewart, Toronto

Produced by Laing Communications Inc.
Redmond, Washington. Design by Sandra J. Harner

Printed in the U.S.A.   First Edition   10 9 8 7 6 5 4 3 2 1

Contents

◆　◆　◆

The first shots of the Civil War were fired at Fort Sumter, a Federal post in Charleston harbor, South Carolina.

INTRODUCTION

War!

◆　　◆　　◆

In 1861, four million black men, women, and children lived as slaves in the United States. The U.S. Constitution left it up to individual states to decide whether to allow slavery, and in the North it had been outlawed for decades. But the South still depended on slaves to plant and harvest the cotton, tobacco, rice and sugar cane from which its wealth came, and slavery there remained legal.

Most Northerners were willing to tolerate slavery in the South, but they were determined to prevent it from spreading to any of the newly forming states in the West. Southerners were just as determined to preserve their right—and the right of people in any other state—to own slaves, even if it meant breaking away from the United States and forming a separate nation. By 1861, eleven states had done just that, pronouncing themselves the Confederate States of America.

Slavery was the foremost among many issues dividing the North and South. The differences, which had been smoldering for years, finally burst into flames in the early morning hours of April 12, 1861, when Confederate troops opened fire on Fort Sumter, a Federal fort in the harbor of Charleston, South Carolina. The Civil War had begun.

Two days later, President Abraham Lincoln called for seventy-five thousand volunteers to join the northern army and crush the rebellion.

Inflamed with anger and pride, thousands of young white men, some no older than fourteen or fifteen, rushed to enlist. Large numbers of black men also answered the call. But while white volunteers were greeted eagerly, black men were turned away.

"We want you d——d niggers to keep out of this," officials told a group of black citizens trying to organize a military company in Cincinnati, Ohio. "This is a white man's war."

Most Northerners believed that the war was being fought only to restore the Union. They simply wanted to bring the eleven southern states back into the United States, even if it meant allowing slavery to continue in those states. But to black Americans, the war was also, inevitably, about ending slavery. And no one had more reason to fight than they.

Frederick Douglass, a prominent abolitionist, writer, and speaker—and former slave—made the case for black enlistment eloquently. "A war undertaken and brazenly carried on for the perpetual enslavement of colored men calls logically and loudly for colored men to help suppress it."

Douglass and other opponents of slavery vowed to persevere until black men were "enlisted and permitted to share the dangers and honor of upholding the government."

But it would be nearly two more years before they won that opportunity. On January 1, 1863, President

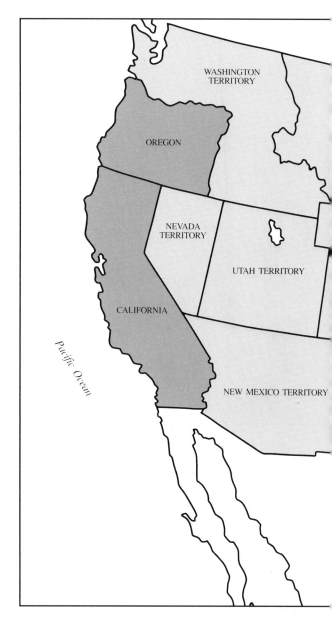

Lincoln issued a proclamation that allowed black men to enlist in the army and declared that all slaves living in the states fighting against the Union were free.

The war that began as a fight to reunite the country had also become a war to free four million slaves. By the time it was over, some 200,000 black men would fight, and nearly 39,000 would die, for that cause.

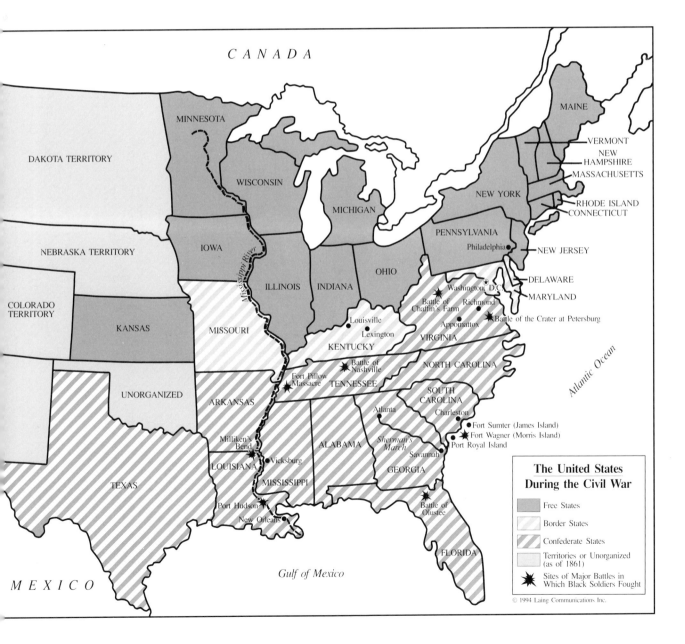

The United States During the Civil War

Although the northern army at first refused to enlist them as soldiers, many black men found ways to help the Union war effort. This man unloaded supplies from ships and ferried them to shore.

ONE

Determined To Serve

♦　　♦　　♦

On April 23, 1861, just nine days after the fall of Fort Sumter, a free black man from Washington, D.C., wrote to U.S. Secretary of War Simon Cameron. In his letter, Jacob Dodson said he knew "of some three hundred . . . reliable colored free citizens of this City, who desire to enter the service for the defence of the City."

During the first year of the Civil War, similar letters poured into the War Department from black citizens living in northern and midwestern states.

G. P. Miller, a black doctor in Battle Creek, Michigan, asked Secretary Cameron's permission to "raise from five thousand to ten thousand free men to report in sixty days."

W. T. Boyd and J. T. Alston of Cleveland, Ohio, asked for the "privilege of fighting—and (if need be dieing)" for the Union cause. They said they could muster a thousand volunteers from their state.

Rufus Sibb Jones, the captain of a black militia company in Pittsburgh, offered the services of his Fort Pitt Cadets. They had been training for two years, Jones said, and were "quite Proficient in military discipline."

The Reverend Garland H. White, a former slave who had escaped to Canada, informed Cameron that he had "a Black regiment [that] offers their services in protection of the southern forts."

The polite and respectful tone of these offers masked the fierce desire of black Americans to fight for the freedom of their people.

But the answer from the War Department was always the same: no. The Union Army did not want the help of black men. The North was in the war to save the Union, not to end slavery.

Besides, there was no need to enlist black soldiers. Union government officials and citizens alike were confident that the northern armies would crush the Confederate rebellion within a few months.

President Abraham Lincoln was morally opposed to slavery, but since the U.S. Constitution protected the right of each state to permit

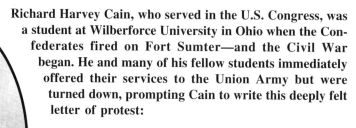

Richard Harvey Cain, who served in the U.S. Congress, was a student at Wilberforce University in Ohio when the Confederates fired on Fort Sumter—and the Civil War began. He and many of his fellow students immediately offered their services to the Union Army but were turned down, prompting Cain to write this deeply felt letter of protest:

I shall never forget the thrill that ran through my soul when I thought of the coming consequences of that shot. There were one hundred and fifteen of us students at the University, who, anxious to vindicate the stars and stripes, made up a company and offered our services to the Governor of Ohio; and sir, we were told that this is a white man's war and that the Negro had nothing to do with it. Sir, we returned, docile, patient, waiting, casting our eyes to the Heavens whence help always comes. We knew that there would come a period in the history of this nation when our strong black arms would be needed. We waited patiently; we waited until Massachusetts, through her noble Governor, sounded the alarm, and we hastened to hear the summons and obey it.

it, he believed he had no legal right to abolish slavery in the states where it already existed. He also wanted to retain the loyalty of the four slave states that had stayed in the Union when the war began— Kentucky, Maryland, Missouri, and Delaware. Those states formed a valuable geographic buffer between the North and the Confederacy. If Lincoln broadened the scope of the war to include ending slavery in the rebel states, the border states might worry that he planned to outlaw slavery in their states as well and shift their allegiance to the Confederacy.

Lincoln repeatedly assured the border states that they were in no danger of losing their human property. "We didn't go into the war to put down slavery," he said, "but to put the flag back."

Free blacks were disheartened by the government's narrow view of the war and its refusal to allow them to serve their country. Some, such as Philadelphian Henry Cropper, became bitter, vowing never to "offer or give service, except it be on equality with all other men."

Disappointed though they might have been, northern black citizens continued to believe that the Civil War *was* about ending slavery and that sooner or later they would be called upon to serve. During the second half of 1861 and well into 1862, they continued to organize, drill, and ready themselves for battle.

Some light-skinned blacks joined the army by pretending to be white. Other blacks helped the Union in any way they could, if only as cooks for white soldiers, servants for white officers, or laborers under white supervisors. Black women, too, offered their services, as laundresses, seamstresses, and nurses.

An editorial published on September 14, 1861, in the *Anglo-African*, a weekly New York newspaper, echoed the views of most free black Americans:

"Talk as we may, we *are* concerned in this fight, and our fate hangs upon its issues. . . . In aiding the Federal government in whatever way we can, we are aiding to secure our own liberty. . . . We do not affirm that the North is fighting in behalf of the black man's rights. . . . [but] that in struggling for their own nationality they are forced to defend our rights."

In the South, too, black men and women were helping the Union cause, mostly as laborers and laundresses, but also as guides and spies. Wherever Union troops pushed into Confederate territory, slaves escaped from plantations to seek refuge and freedom in the Yankee camps.

In those early days of the war, the government's policy was not to interfere with rebels' property, human or otherwise. Camp commanders were advised to send runaway slaves back to their owners. In keeping with the policy, many Union commanders allowed slaveowners to enter their camps to seize their escaped slaves.

Other officers ordered their troops to return fugitive slaves to their masters. When one of his junior officers arrived back from a raiding party into northern Virginia accompanied by six slaves he had rescued from a local plantation, Colonel D. S. Miles ordered the officer to "send [the slaves] back to the farm."

A fair number of northern commanders were appalled by the idea of forcing runaway slaves, who had risked so much to escape, to return to bondage. These men explicitly forbade their troops to send fugitives back, and openly discouraged slaveholders from entering their camps to retrieve runaways.

Colonel Josiah W. Bissell found a foolproof way to frustrate any slaveowner who came to his camp hunting for an escaped slave. After hiding the runaway in an officer's tent, Bissell would ask one of his men to escort the slaveowner through the camp, allowing him to search everywhere. When they reached the tent harboring the fugitive, the guide would tell the slaveowner that the man inside, a "Captain Hill," had developed symptoms of smallpox. That announcement invariably ended the search and the slaveowner returned home empty-handed.

Along with providing food and shelter for fugitive slaves, officers

"Why does the Government reject the Negro: Is he not a man? Can he not wield a sword, fire a gun, march and countermarch, and obey orders like any other . . . ?" No one argued more forcefully for black enlistment than Frederick Douglass, former slave, abolitionist, and black leader. He spoke to large gatherings throughout the North and ran passionate editorials in his newspaper, *Douglass' Monthly.*

These escaped slaves found safety with Union troops at Yorktown, Virginia, where the women went to work washing soldiers' clothes.

such as Bissell often put them to work. The men did everything from cooking and digging latrines to loading supply wagons and building fortifications. Women did laundry and mended torn uniforms. By using escaped slaves to perform these mundane but essential noncombat tasks, the officers reasoned, they could free up more white troops for fighting.

Before long, even men such as Colonel Miles, who at first opposed giving sanctuary to runaway slaves, came to see black laborers as indispensable. Congress also recognized their contribution to the war effort and passed laws making it illegal for Union officers to return the slaves of disloyal men to their owners.

Even as the army came to depend on fugitive slave labor, the Union still was not ready to accept black men as soldiers. The majority of white Northerners, although uncomfortable with the idea of one person owning another, did not believe in racial equality.

Many were just as prejudiced as the average Southerner. Black Americans were not allowed to vote in most free states and were banned from white churches and public facilities. Black children were barred from attending school with white children.

Most Northerners simply did not believe that black men were smart enough, skilled enough, or brave enough to make good soldiers. Allowing them to join the army would almost be like admitting they were equal to white men. Few white Americans could accept such a notion.

At least three powerful and independent-minded Northerners took a different stand. Defying federal policy, these three men—two generals and a United States senator—recruited, trained, and sent into battle hundreds of black soldiers as early as the fall of 1861.

In May 1862, Major General David Hunter, commander of Union-held territory in the Sea Islands along the coast of South Carolina, began recruiting for an all-black unit. His efforts did not go smoothly. Many of the slaves living on the islands had no desire to join the army. Their masters had fled the approaching Union forces, leaving them "free" for the first time in their lives to farm the land and live as they pleased. When only a handful signed up voluntarily, the impatient commander instructed his recruiters to take men by force.

Adding to Hunter's troubles, the War Department turned down his request for

Hundreds of runaway slaves sought refuge at Fortress Monroe in Virginia. The fort's commander, Union General Benjamin Butler, called the fugitives "contraband of war" and refused to send them back to their owners.

money to pay the troops and for authorization to commission white officers. Government officials were not about to reward this upstart, who, after all, had raised a black regiment without their approval. Hunter was forced to disband the First South Carolina Colored Volunteers just three months after forming the regiment. When the unit was reorganized a few months later, this time with full War Department support, islanders' memories of Hunter's harsh treatment made recruiting difficult.

Like Hunter, General John W. Phelps was ahead of the Lincoln administration in his readiness to enlist black men. In charge of Camp Parapet, Louisiana, a post a few miles from New Orleans, Phelps set out to organize several companies of black soldiers.

Unlike Hunter, Phelps did not resort to strong-arm tactics. But he had no more luck in persuading the government to recognize the regiment as part of the army.

Instead, Phelps's commanders ordered him to put the former slaves in his camp to good use, "cutting timber and building fortifications." Unwilling to accept orders he felt would make him little better than a slavedriver, Phelps resigned from the army and went home to Vermont.

Senator James Lane of Kansas flouted government policy on arming black men even earlier than Phelps and Hunter. In the fall of

Their clothes torn and tattered after a long, hazardous journey to Union lines, these two young escaped slaves probably found work as servants or cooks for Union officers.

1861, the senator began enlisting runaway slaves into the Union cavalry. When he received a War Department commission in the summer of 1862 to raise troops for the army, Lane assumed he was free to recruit white *and* black volunteers. He placed advertisements in newspapers statewide urging black men to join his ranks.

Since Kansas, a free state, had only a small black population, Lane sent recruiting agents to every northern state to find enlistees. He also encouraged slaves from neighboring Missouri to escape across the border to Kansas. By the end of October, he had filled two black regiments—the First and Second Kansas Colored Volunteers.

Early in the war, Union commanders could not enlist blacks as soldiers, but they put them to work behind the lines building stockades, digging latrines, and performing other noncombat tasks.

When Secretary of War Edwin Stanton (who had replaced Simon Cameron) heard what Lane was doing, he cabled the senator that he was not "authorized to organize . . . any but loyal white men." Lane ignored the telegram and kept right on drilling black soldiers and

Celebrating Freedom

The first day of 1863 dawned cold and bright at Camp Saxton on Port Royal Island, South Carolina. The soldiers of the First South Carolina Colored Volunteers proudly donned their bright blue coats and scarlet pantaloons, carefully washed and pressed for the celebration.

There was to be a program of prayers, hymns, and speeches, highlighted by a reading of President Lincoln's Emancipation Proclamation. In the evening, there would be a great feast of roasted oxen, hard bread, and molasses.

By ten o'clock, great numbers of freedmen, women, and children had begun arriving at the camp, most of them ferried by steamer from surrounding islands. The freed people were dressed in their holiday best, recalled northern teacher Charlotte Forten, with "the gayest of head-handkerchiefs, the whitest of aprons, and the happiest of faces." There were five thousand visitors in all, including northern missionaries and teachers, and officers from other Union regiments.

Following the reading of the proclamation, the camp chaplain presented the regimental flag to Colonel Thomas Wentworth Higginson, the commander of the First South Carolina Colored Volunteers. Higginson later recalled how, as he waved the flag, "there suddenly arose, close beside the platform, a strong male voice . . . into which two women's voices instantly blended, singing, as if by an impulse that could no more be repressed than the morning note of the song-sparrow:

> *My Country, 'tis of thee,*
> *Sweet land of liberty,*
> *Of thee I sing.*

"People looked at each other," recalled Higginson, "and then at us on the platform, to see whence came this interruption, not set down in the [program]. Firmly and irrepressibly, the quavering voices sang on, verse after verse; others of the colored people joined in.

"I never saw anything so electric," the colonel wrote. "It made all other words cheap; it seemed the choked voice of a race at last unloosed. . . . Just think of it! The first day they had ever had a country, the first flag they had ever seen which promised anything to

sending them into battle. A year later, the War Department grudgingly admitted Lane's two black regiments into the Union Army.

Stories about the actions of these three men—and of the skill and bravery of the black troops—spread throughout the North. At the same

The flag bearers of the First South Carolina Colored Volunteers join in the New Year's Day celebration of freedom on Port Royal Island, South Carolina.

their people. . . . When they stopped, there was nothing to do for it but to speak, and I went on; but the life of the whole day was in those unknown people's song."

After his speech, Higginson passed the flag to his color guard, Sergeant Prince Rivers and Corporal Robert Sutton. The two soldiers encouraged the black men in the crowd "to enlist and fight for their friends and relatives still in bondage." Once the ceremony was over, the men of the First South Carolina Colored Volunteers demonstrated their prowess in a dress parade, "a brilliant and beautiful sight," wrote Charlotte Forten.

When the celebration was over, Susie King Taylor, whose husband was a soldier with the South Carolina regiment, summed up the feelings of soldiers and civilians alike: "It was a glorious day for us all."

By the time President Abraham Lincoln issued the Emancipation Proclamation on January 1, 1863, he had come to believe that freeing the slaves was the best way to undermine the Confederates and assure a Union victory.

time, grim reports of Union defeats dominated news headlines. The Confederate Army had surprised the experts who said the South could not put up a serious fight. The war that was expected to last only a few months had become an endless nightmare of bloodshed and death. By 1862, both sides had lost tens of thousands of men to battle, disease, injury, desertion, or discharge.

The number of Union volunteers, meanwhile, had slowed to a trickle. A year earlier, young men had flooded the enlistment stations, anxious to share in the glory of what promised to be a speedy victory. But their enthusiasm faded as they read the weekly casualty lists and saw friends and relatives return home with horrible wounds, often having lost an arm or leg.

As they considered these issues, many white Northerners began to rethink the role black men could play in the war. Enlisting them as soldiers could solve the growing manpower shortage. And, if black men joined up in large numbers, fewer white men would have to fight and die.

President Lincoln's views were changing, too. There was no denying that black laborers had become indispensable to the army. Perhaps enrolling black men as soldiers would hasten the end of this awful war. On August 25, 1862, Lincoln ordered Secretary of War Stanton to begin recruiting black troops in the Sea Islands.

Lincoln's thinking about the connection between the war and ending slavery had also changed. By mid-1862, he was convinced that the only way to assure Union victory was to liberate all slaves in the rebel states. The loss of its labor force would cripple the Confederate economy and force white men who would otherwise join the rebel army to work in the fields.

In September, the president put the Confederacy on alert. Unless the rebellious states rejoined the Union by the end of the year, he would issue an Emancipation Proclamation declaring all slaves free. (The proclamation would not affect slavery in the loyal border states.)

It was often Union soldiers who delivered the news of freedom to slaves on southern plantations. In this idealized painting, a slave family listens raptly as a soldier reads the Emancipation Proclamation.

Lincoln's ultimatum only angered Confederates, who had no intention of giving up after two years of fighting, especially at a time when the war seemed to be going their way. None of the Confederate states heeded Lincoln's warning.

On New Year's Day, the president delivered his promised proclamation, affirming that all slaves in the rebel states were "forever free." Joined by their abolitionist supporters, black men and women throughout the North and South rejoiced.

The proclamation that freed the slaves also authorized the recruitment of black men as Union soldiers. After nearly two years of struggle, black Americans had finally won the chance to fight for the Union—and for freedom.

COME AND JOIN US BROTHERS.

Army recruiters used brightly colored posters featuring fully equipped black soldiers and inspirational messages to encourage free black men to join up.

TWO

Men of Color, to Arms!

◆   ◆   ◆

The three Wilson brothers were slaves on a plantation in Savannah, Georgia, when word reached them that a company of black soldiers was being organized near Port Royal Island, South Carolina. The brothers made plans to run away and sign up. They knew escaping would be dangerous, but they were willing to risk their lives to reach Union lines and freedom.

Every night for months, the men took turns sneaking down to the riverbank near their shack on the plantation. There, hidden in the brush, was a big log they were painstakingly hollowing out. It would make a fine canoe, strong enough to carry the men, their sister, and her nine-year-old daughter along the inland waterways of Georgia across the border to Port Royal.

The trip was even more hazardous than the family had feared. All the way from Savannah to Port Royal, the woods on both sides of the rivers were filled with rebels who fired at the runaways as they floated past in their dugout, unable to defend themselves. By the time the family was taken aboard a Union gunboat patrolling near Port Royal, all three brothers had been shot at least once. After recovering from their wounds, the men joined the First South Carolina Colored Volunteers.

Many slaves living near the water escaped by boat—sometimes their own, sometimes stolen—and rowed miles to the nearest Union Army camp.

Like the Wilsons, most of the men who volunteered for black Union regiments organized in the occupied South were runaway slaves. By 1862, large numbers of escaped slaves were living in what were called contraband camps, which sprang up everywhere Union troops penetrated Confederate territory—South Carolina, Louisiana, Mississippi, Virginia, Tennessee, and North Carolina. After the Union committed itself to enlisting black soldiers, these camps proved a ready source of new recruits.

Most runaway slaves grabbed at the chance to fight for freedom for themselves and loved ones still in slavery. Assurances of regular pay and protection for their families made the army's offer even more compelling.

If Union commanders ran short of suitable volunteers from among contraband camps, they sent recruiting parties—often five to ten black soldiers led by a white officer—into nearby southern towns and plantations. There, they rounded up all the field workers and house servants and urged the military-age men (roughly, those eighteen to forty-five years old) to join the fight for freedom. Recruiters promised the men that their wives and children could come with them to the Union camps, where they would be fed, clothed, and protected. Deeply moved by the sight of black men in army uniforms and by the recruiters' passionate words about liberation, most slaves eagerly signed on.

Not surprisingly, the slaves' owners were infuriated by the raids. Lincoln's Emancipation Proclamation may have declared their slaves free, but Confederates did not feel bound by Union laws or proclamations. The fact that it was black soldiers who were so brazenly stealing their work force made the slaveholders angrier still. But most were intimidated by the presence of well-armed troops and confined their protests to shouting threats from the safety of their front porches. Others, when they heard that recruiters were coming, hid all their slave men and teenage boys.

Not all slaveowners were afraid of the Union soldiers. In Kentucky, several recruiting agents were "caught, stripped, tied to a tree and cowhided," then chased out of town. Another agent, a white lieutenant leading a recruiting party through western Maryland, was murdered by slaveowners intent on keeping their work force.

Thousands of slaves also were recruited by Union troops that swept through Confederate territory on foraging expeditions to gather food, lumber, livestock, and other supplies. One such expedition went up the Combahee River in South Carolina in 1863. Slaves working in the rice plantations along the river were terrified when they first saw the strange iron-covered boats moving toward them. But as word spread that these were "Lincoln's gun-boats come to

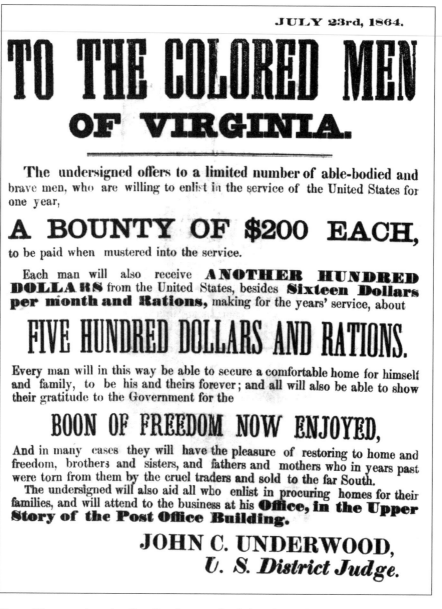

JULY 23rd, 1864.

TO THE COLORED MEN
OF VIRGINIA.

The undersigned offers to a limited number of able-bodied and brave men, who are willing to enlist in the service of the United States for one year,

A BOUNTY OF $200 EACH,

to be paid when mustered into the service.

Each man will also receive **ANOTHER HUNDRED DOLLARS** from the United States, besides **Sixteen Dollars per month and Rations,** making for the years' service, about

FIVE HUNDRED DOLLARS AND RATIONS.

Every man will in this way be able to secure a comfortable home for himself and family, to be his and theirs forever; and all will also be able to show their gratitude to the Government for the

BOON OF FREEDOM NOW ENJOYED,

And in many cases they will have the pleasure of restoring to home and freedom, brothers and sisters, and fathers and mothers who in years past were torn from them by the cruel traders and sold to the far South.

The undersigned will also aid all who enlist in procuring homes for their families, and will attend to the business at his **Office, in the Upper Story of the Post Office Building.**

JOHN C. UNDERWOOD,
U. S. District Judge.

Recruiting posters in the South promised freedom, full pay, and bounties to attract former slaves to Union service.

set them free," eight hundred slaves, braving the whips of over-
seers, raced to the river and piled onto the boats.

By the spring of 1863, recruiting raids on Confederate soil had
become standard Union policy. Still, many Union field commanders grumbled at having to use their men for such a purpose. Gen-
eral-in-Chief of the Army Henry W. Halleck pointed out to the
officers that there was no surer way to help the Union *and* hurt the

Stealing the *Planter*

Born into slavery on Port Royal Island in South Carolina,
Robert Smalls worked on boats from early childhood. When
the Civil War broke out, Smalls was twenty-two years old
and a deckhand on the *Planter*, a cotton steamer based
in Charleston harbor. He earned sixteen dollars a month,
but as a slave was only allowed to keep a dollar; the
rest went to his owner.

Late in 1861, the Confederate Army leased the
Planter and its black crew to transport ammunition, guns,
and food to rebel forts along the coast. Smalls's knowledge
of local waterways impressed the white officers who took
command of the ship, and they soon promoted him to
pilot. (Unwilling to give a slave such an important
title, the officers referred to him as the "wheelman.")

Even though he held a position of responsibility,
Smalls was still a slave. In the spring of 1862, the
Union captured Port Royal and the other Sea Islands,
located just a few miles beyond Charleston harbor.
All of the landowners fled, leaving their slaves the
only occupants of the plantations. Smalls grew
restless knowing freedom was so close—so close, in fact, that as he
walked the decks of the *Planter* peering through the captain's field
glasses, he could see the Union blockade fleet anchored just outside
the harbor. The sight inspired him to plan a daring escape.

For weeks, Smalls and his eight crewmates waited for their chance.
It finally came on the night of May 12, when the white captain,
engineer, and mate left the ship to attend a ball at Fort Sumter hosted by
the wealthy society families of Charleston. They would not be back
before dawn.

At three o'clock in the morning, Smalls ordered the men to start the

Robert Smalls

Confederacy than by drawing slaves into Union ranks: "So long as the rebels retain and employ their slaves in producing grains," he argued, "they can employ all the whites in the [battle]field." Every slave Union recruiters took off a plantation, Halleck continued, meant one less laborer for the Confederacy and one more man for the Union.

Large numbers of slaves from the border states of Maryland,

---

engine and cast off. Even at that usually quiet hour, they faced a perilous journey. Between the *Planter* and its destination—the Union fleet—were six heavily armed forts. Only by giving the proper signal—a secret combination of short and long blasts from the ship's whistle—would Smalls and his crew be allowed to pass. Danger lurked below the water as well, where deadly mines floated, ready to blow up any invading Union ship. But Smalls was prepared. He had been watching and waiting for weeks, and had learned all the signals and memorized the exact location of every mine.

Smalls expertly eased the *Planter* away from the dock. His first stop was the North Atlantic wharf, a few miles away, where the crew's wives and children were waiting by prearrangement. They picked up the five women and three children without incident and continued on to the most treacherous leg of their journey, past the forts.

To avoid raising rebel suspicions, Smalls raised the ship's two flags—Confederate and state—and kept the *Planter* to a moderate speed. He even put on the captain's straw hat and jacket and mimicked his walk as he moved about the deck. As the ship passed each fort, Smalls confidently gave the correct signal.

Once in open sea, Smalls ordered the crew to open the engine full throttle, run a white sheet up the flag pole as a sign of surrender, and make for the nearest Union ship—the *Onward*.

"Good morning, sir!" shouted Smalls as he maneuvered the *Planter* alongside the Union warship. "I've brought some of the old United States guns, sir!"

The *Onward*'s captain received the *Planter* crew warmly. Smalls had not only delivered him a Confederate ship, but her valuable cargo as well: two hundred pounds of ammunition and four big guns that had been loaded on the ship the night before the men made their escape.

Smalls's remarkable feat marked the beginning of a distinguished career in the service of his country; he piloted Union ships throughout the war and was promoted to honorary captain in December 1863. After the war, Smalls was elected to the South Carolina Legislature and to the U.S. Congress.

Missouri, and Kentucky also ran away to join the army. This posed a problem for President Lincoln. Although he wanted to enlist slaves in the rebel states, he had promised slaveholders in the loyal border states that their slaves would not be recruited.

Even if he had known about the bargain struck between President Lincoln and border state slaveowners, Kentucky slave Elijah Marrs would not have cared. He cared only about freedom, and joining the Union Army was his best chance of getting it. In the fall of 1864, he began planning his escape from Simpsonville to the Union recruiting station in nearby Louisville. When other local slaves learned that Marrs, who was widely admired for his ability to read and write, was going to join the Union Army, they asked if they

Once they reached Union lines, escaped slaves signed enlistment papers and underwent medical examinations.

could go with him. Twenty-seven men decided to join Marrs and elected him their "captain."

Over a twenty-four-hour period, the men worked out their escape plans in a local black church as their families and friends looked on. At one point, panic swept through the gathering when word spread that the rebels were in town "preparing to make a raid upon the church," recalled Marrs. "Women screamed, jumped out the windows . . . strong men ran pell-mell over the women and took to the woods." Marrs, too, debated whether to "throw up the sponge," but "picked up courage" and rallied his men. News soon came that the report of a rebel attack was false.

Nevertheless, Marrs and his men hurried their meeting. "The conclusion of the boys was," said Marrs, "that where I would lead they would follow. I said to them that we might as well go; that if we staid at home, we would be murdered; that if we joined the army and were slain in battle, we would at least die in fighting for principle and freedom."

When night fell, the local minister preached a farewell sermon. "It was known by nearly every one present that night that there were a number of young men in the house who were preparing to leave for the army . . . consequently there was great weeping and mourning," Marrs said. Finally, all the goodbyes were said.

Marrs led his men two miles to the shack where he grew up. His Aunt Beller gave them something to eat, while Marrs went inside and collected two hundred of the three hundred dollars he had managed to save during slavery; he left the rest for his mother.

By 11:00 P.M., the group was back on the march. The most dangerous part of the journey lay ahead—Middletown, a town "through which the colored people seldom passed with safety." Circling to the left of town, the company bypassed Middletown without incident. The men had just returned to the main road when they heard "the rumbling of vehicles coming at full speed, as we supposed, toward us."

Armed only with "twenty-six war clubs and one pistol," the fugitives were ill-prepared to defend themselves. In a flash, Marrs ordered his men to throw themselves down and lie flat in a ditch beside the road. They remained there, barely daring to breathe, for twenty-five minutes before deciding it was safe to continue.

As dawn broke on September 26, 1864, the men reached Union

lines. "By eight o'clock," reported Marrs, "we were at the recruiting office in the city of Louisville. . . . By twelve o'clock the owner of every man of us was in the city hunting his slaves, but we had all enlisted save one boy, who was considered too young." Marrs was assigned to Company L of the Twelfth U.S. Colored Heavy Artillery and soon was promoted to sergeant.

Like Elijah Marrs, Kentucky slaves escaped by the thousands to Union camps within the state and across the border into the free states of Ohio, Indiana, and Illinois, where they joined black regiments. Fugitives from Maryland made their way to Washington, D.C., where slavery had been outlawed since 1862. Missouri slaves fled across the borders to Kansas and Illinois.

The trip was always difficult and filled with risks. During the day, runaways hid in cellars, barns, and swamps, or, if they were lucky, in the homes of southern abolitionists or free blacks. At night, they crept through woods and along back roads to avoid detection, often traveling as many as twenty miles before resting.

When large numbers of border state slaves began arriving at their camps, Union officers were reluctant to enlist them for fear of upsetting slaveholders. But recruiting among free black men in those states did not yield enough soldiers and angered slaveowners who saw *any* recruitment in their states as a threat.

Eventually, the Union Army's desperate need for more troops won out over the desire to retain the allegiance of border state slaveholders. In October 1863, the War Department issued a policy allowing slaves in those states to enlist if they had their master's permission. If judged loyal to the Union, the slaveowners would be paid for the loss of their slaves. Recognizing that few owners would willingly give up their slaves—even with compensation—to fight a war that would end slavery, the government also allowed slaves to join without permission.

This decision signaled the beginning of the end of slavery in the border states. As more and more slaves exchanged bondage for freedom, slavery lost its hold. In November 1864, Maryland lawmakers passed a new constitution abolishing slavery in the state; two months later, Missouri did the same. (Kentucky remained a slave state until December 1865 when the Thirteenth Amendment to the U.S. Constitution outlawed slavery nationwide.)

Twenty-two-year-old Private Hubbard Pryor, before and after he joined the Forty-fourth U.S. Colored Infantry in 1864

Whether they lived in the border states or the occupied South, slaveowners often went to extremes to prevent their slaves from escaping to join the army. On a recruiting trip through Prince Georges County, Maryland, Colonel Joseph Perkins discovered twenty slaves in a local jail. The jailer told Perkins, who was an officer with a black regiment, that the slaves' owners had locked them in the jail early in the war to prevent them from running away.

You Have No Choice!

Free or slave, not all black men wanted to go to war. Some could not bear to leave their families and friends. Some did not want to risk their lives. Some slaves feared their owners might retaliate against their families, and some free black men were earning better wages than they could make in the army.

But as the war dragged on and the need for men grew, army recruiters became less and less sensitive to the feelings of reluctant "volunteers." Throughout the South and sometimes in the North, black men were impressed—or forced—into the military.

As stories circulated about Union raiding parties "descending upon towns and plantations in the dead of night" and carrying men off to nearby military camps, many black men tried to escape the recruiters' net. They hid deep in the woods, slept under their beds, even crawled up chimneys. "Not a man sleeps at night in the houses," reported a white missionary. "They have a camp somewhere and mean never to be caught."

Some Union officers coerced black men into joining the army. One admitted locking a man in a guardhouse for three days to "persuade him." A northern missionary working in Portsmouth, Virginia, reported to General Benjamin Butler that Union soldiers under the command of Colonel John A. Nelson were daily taking "Colored Citizens . . . from their houses, workshops [wagons], churches and schools" to Craney Island "where they are urged to enlist." Any men who refused, wrote the missionary, were "forced to carry a ball, supposed to weigh forty or fifty pounds" for several hours.

Armistead Lewis, a free black man from Zenia, Ohio, was walking home from church one Sunday when a Union guard demanded his pass. Lewis handed it over, but the guard refused to give it back,

In one room, Perkins found a dozen women and children. In another, he discovered eight men in leg irons. Each man was shackled by a chain to one "large staple in the middle of the room." Perkins called for a blacksmith to release the men. After they were free, he enlisted the male slaves on the spot and escorted the entire group, including the women and children, back to his camp.

Some plantation owners locked up their slaves' clothes and shoes at night. Others tried to scare them into staying by telling stories

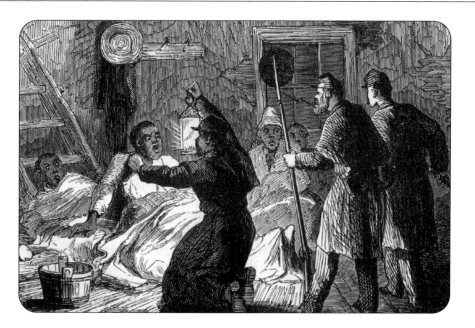

Not all black men were eager to join the army, but few could escape the determined recruiters who stormed into their homes and carried them off to enlistment stations.

ordering him to "fall in" with the guard and his men. "I was marched around from place to place till they collected all they could get [180 men]," said Lewis. The guards "took the passes of the men and . . . burned them before us," not wanting to leave any evidence of their illegal recruitment. Any man who tried to leave, the guards warned, would be shot.

The War Department frowned on these practices, but could do little to stop them, and recruiters continued to enlist black—and white—soldiers by force.

of the terrible fate that awaited slaves who joined the army: Officers would put them on the front lines to draw enemy fire away from white soldiers; they would treat them cruelly and never pay them; and even worse, if taken prisoner by rebels, they would be hanged. Any black soldier who survived the war, slaveowners cautioned, would be sold back into slavery.

Yankees were monstrous creatures, one plantation owner told slave children. Each had a great horn growing out of his forehead and a single eye in the middle of his chest. Another owner warned her slaves that the Yankees planned to kill every "nigger in the South." Such predictions were usually outright lies and always exaggerated. But, as later events would show, there was a grain of truth in some of the tales.

Punishment was severe for slaves caught attempting to escape to Union lines. In Kentucky, white men cut off the left ears of two slaves who had run away to enlist. Aaron Mitchell of Missouri, a man named Alfred, and two other slaves were caught soon after they set out for a recruiting station in Hannibal. All four were severely whipped. But Alfred's owner was not satisfied with a beating. Turning to a group of whites who had been watching, she offered five dollars to any man who would kill the runaway. Without hesitation, an onlooker stepped forward, coolly shot Alfred through the heart, and collected his five dollars.

When they could not frighten their slaves into staying, angry slaveowners often took revenge on family members the men had left behind.

For thousands of slaves, the pull of freedom was far stronger than the fear of capture and punishment. Altogether, some 100,000 black men joined the Union Army from the parts of the South occupied by northern troops. Another 42,000 joined from the border states.

In the free states of the North, it was often black ministers and businessmen who led efforts to create and fill regiments. They organized mass meetings, gave speeches, and tirelessly distributed broadsides and flyers urging young men to serve. Black newspapers ran stirring editorials.

"Shame on him who would hang back at the call of his country," declared the *Christian Recorder*, a Philadelphia newspaper

VOLUNTEER ENLISTMENT.

STATE OF *Tennessee*   TOWN OF *Murfreesboro*

I, *Edmund Wort* born in *Davidson County* in the State of *Tennessee* aged *twenty-eight* years, and by occupation a *Farmer*, Do HEREBY ACKNOWLEDGE to have volunteered this *twenty-fifth* day of *September* 1863 to serve as a *Soldier* in the Army of the United States of America, for the period of *THREE YEARS*, unless sooner discharged by proper authority: Do also agree to accept such bounty, pay, rations, and clothing, as are, or may be, established by law for volunteers. And I, *Edmund Wort* do solemnly swear, that I will bear true faith and allegiance to the **United States of America,** and that I will serve them honestly and faithfully against all their enemies or opposers whomsoever; and that I will observe and obey the orders of the President of the United States, and the orders of the officers appointed over me, according to the Rules and Articles of War.

Sworn and subscribed to, at this   day of   18 . }   Edmund + Wort — his mark

I CERTIFY, ON HONOR, That I have carefully examined the above named Volunteer, agreeably to the General Regulations of the Army, and that in my opinion he is free from all bodily defects and mental infirmity, which would, in any way, disqualify him from performing the duties of a soldier.

Charles M. Baum

EXAMINING SURGEON.

I CERTIFY, ON HONOR, That I have minutely inspected the Volunteer, previously to his enlistment, and that he was entirely sober when enlisted; that, to the best of my judgment and belief, he is of lawful age; and that, in accepting him as duly qualified to perform the duties of an able-bodied soldier, I have strictly observed the Regulations which govern the recruiting service. This soldier has *black* eyes, *black* hair, *yellow* complexion, is *five feet eight inches* high.

Second Regiment *U.S. Colored* Volunteers,

GOV. PRINT. OFF. July, 1862.   RECRUITING OFFICER.

Like most black soldiers, twenty-eight-year-old Edmund Wort agreed to serve in the Union Army for three years.

published by a prominent black church. "Go with the view that you will return freemen. And if you should never return, you will die with the satisfaction of knowing that you have struck a blow for freedom, and assisted in giving liberty to our race."

The Reverend Garland H. White, whose first offer to raise a black regiment had been turned down by the War Department, recruited men "for every colored regiment raised" in the North and West. As a reward for his services, White, who enlisted in the Twenty-eighth U.S. Colored Infantry, was promoted to chaplain of the regiment in 1864. (He was one of thirteen black soldiers who were commissioned as chaplains during the Civil War,

Their Own Call to Arms

Countless black women helped the Union Army—and the fight for freedom—in any way they could. Not allowed to serve as soldiers, they worked as teachers, nurses, laundresses, cooks, and also as spies and scouts.

One of the best known of these women was Harriet Tubman, an escaped slave. Tubman helped more than three hundred slaves reach freedom in the northern United States and Canada during the 1850s via the "Underground Railroad," the secret network of abolitionists who fed and sheltered runaway slaves on their treacherous trip north.

Starting in 1862, Tubman also cared for sick and wounded soldiers in military hospitals in the Carolinas and Florida.

Her most important army role was as a scout for Union officers who raided enemy territory to gather equipment and supplies and liberate slaves. Wrapping her head in a bandanna and disguising herself as an old slave woman (although she was only in her forties at the time), Tubman moved easily through rebel territory without drawing attention. She collected information on the location of cotton warehouses, ammunition depots, food stores, and livestock, and passed it on to Union officers. Whenever she encountered young slave men, she urged them to run away and join the Union Army.

Another black woman who

Harriet Tubman was a scout and informant for Union forces.

a rank equivalent to a major in terms of pay, but with no authority on the battlefield.)

In Massachusetts, black leaders had a powerful ally in Governor John A. Andrew. A fierce opponent of slavery, Andrew was one of the first governors to seek War Department approval to

dedicated herself to the Union cause was Sojourner Truth. Deeply religious, an abolitionist and an early feminist, Truth distributed gift boxes of much-appreciated food and clothing to black troops in northern camps. She raised the money to buy these necessities by giving lectures and singing songs to northern audiences.

Truth escaped from slavery in 1827, the year before it was abolished in her home state of New York. In the 1840s, she became deeply involved with the abolitionist movement and vowed to spend the rest of her life traveling and spreading the truth about slavery.

One of the most daring black women to aid the Union cause was Mary Elizabeth Bowser. She served as a spy for the North while working for Confederate President Jefferson Davis.

Sojourner Truth devoted her life to fighting slavery.

Bowser was born a slave in Virginia but was freed as a young woman. Her employer, Elizabeth Van Lew, was the leader of Union supporters in Richmond, Virginia. When Van Lew asked Bowser if she would be willing to be placed in the Confederate president's house as a spy, she agreed and obtained a job as a servant.

As she dusted and swept, Bowser quickly scanned any telegrams and orders that had been left lying about; no one in the household knew she could read. While serving dinner to President Davis and his guests, she listened closely for information about troop movements and other rebel plans. Everything Bowser learned, she passed along to Van Lew, who then conveyed it to Union General Ulysses S. Grant.

organize a northern black regiment. Andrew's recruiting agents placed the following advertisement in a Boston newspaper:

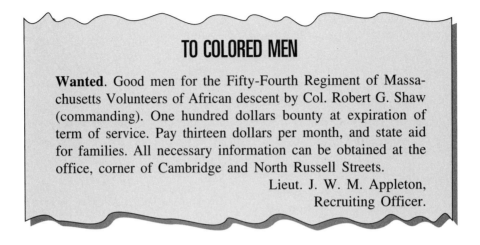

TO COLORED MEN

Wanted. Good men for the Fifty-Fourth Regiment of Massachusetts Volunteers of African descent by Col. Robert G. Shaw (commanding). One hundred dollars bounty at expiration of term of service. Pay thirteen dollars per month, and state aid for families. All necessary information can be obtained at the office, corner of Cambridge and North Russell Streets.

Lieut. J. W. M. Appleton,
Recruiting Officer.

Free black men from around the state responded. But there were not enough black men of military age in Massachusetts to fill a standard thousand-man infantry regiment.

Andrew solved this problem by hiring well-known northern black leaders to act as recruiting agents. He also sought assistance from the most eminent black American of the day, Frederick Douglass. Douglass traveled throughout the North, making speeches to black audiences in which he challenged young men to "get at the throat of treason and slavery" by enlisting in the Fifty-fourth. His own sons, twenty-two-year-old Lewis and nineteen-year-old Charles, were among the first to respond to his appeal.

In his highly charged talks, Douglass echoed the sentiments of many northern blacks. They might have escaped slavery, obtained an education, and made a life for themselves in the North, he told his listeners. But they—and their children—were still treated like second-class citizens.

Serving in the army offered them a chance not only to strike a blow at slavery but also to establish their equality with white Americans. "The iron gate of our prison stands half open," Douglass said in one speech. "The chance is now given you to end in a day the bondage of centuries, and to rise in one bound from social degradation to the place of equality with other varieties of common men."

Thanks in part to ceaseless efforts by men such as Frederick Douglass, the Fifty-fourth Massachusetts had its thousand men by the end of April 1863, just three months after recruiting began. In fact, so many volunteers came forward that Governor Andrew had to organize a second black regiment, the Fifty-fifth Massachusetts.

Many of the men from out-of-state who joined the two Massachusetts regiments would have preferred to serve in a unit raised from their own state. Black men from other free states pressed their governors to seek permission from the War Department. Soon regiments were formed in Ohio, Pennsylvania, Michigan, Iowa, Wisconsin, Illinois, and Indiana. By the end of the war, up to thirty-three thousand northern black men had joined the Union ranks.

Until the spring of 1863, black regiments were raised in a somewhat haphazard fashion by governors or citizen committees in the free states, and by army officers in the occupied South and border states. But in May, the War Department created the U.S. Bureau of Colored Troops

Among the first recruits to join the Fifty-fourth Massachusetts were Frederick Douglass's sons: Sergeant Lewis H. Douglass (left) and Charles R. Douglass. Twenty-two-year-old Lewis fought with distinction at Fort Wagner, where he was one of the few men to reach the top of the enemy fortifications—and survive. Charles, who was nineteen when he enlisted, fought with the Fifty-fourth until 1864, when he was transferred to a Maryland regiment because of poor health.

to oversee all black recruitment and commission officers to lead black regiments.

Wherever or however they joined, black men experienced profound changes once they put on the blue uniform of the Union soldier. It was not the clothes themselves that made the difference; the typical uniform was no more than a simple jacket, a pair of pants, a cap, and a belt. It was what wearing the uniform symbolized—dignity, respect, and equality.

"This is the biggest thing that ever happened in my life," said one former slave. "I felt like a man with a uniform on." Standing at attention during his first roll call as an enlisted man, Elijah Marrs

Black men had fought hard for the right to wear the Union blue, and they wore the uniforms with pride.

said he could feel "freedom in my bones."

One white officer of a black regiment said his troops, all former slaves, were proud to be "recognized as soldiers in the same uniform that white soldiers wear, with the menial service of serfdom forever buried." They felt themselves "lifted to a higher plane, worthy to be the country's defender."

White soldiers, too, noticed the difference. "Put a United States uniform on his back and the *chattel* is a *man*," said one. "You can see it in his look. Between the toiling slave and the soldier is a gulf that nothing but a god could lift him over. He feels it, his looks show it."

Writing in his diary in the last days of 1863, Christian A. Fleetwood, a free black man from Baltimore, expressed the feelings of many. "This year has brought about many changes that at the beginning were or would have been thought impossible. The close of this year finds me a soldier for the cause of my race. May God bless the cause, and enable me in the coming year to forward it on."

For all the pride they felt in their achievement, Fleetwood and thousands of other new black recruits soon discovered that becoming a soldier was no guarantee of equality, and that not all of their fights would take place on the battlefield.

No matter what their experience or how well they performed on the battle-field, black soldiers were denied the chance to serve as commissioned officers until the last few months of the war. Until then, all black regiments were led by white officers.

THREE

Fighting on Two Fronts

◆ ◆ ◆

A s Lieutenant Robert Isabelle signed his name to the Union enlistment form, he looked forward to serving in an army where he was certain "all past prejudice would be suspended for the good of our Country and that all . . . Americans would unite together to sacrifice their blood for the cause."

But Isabelle soon discovered that racial prejudice was just as pervasive in the military as it was in civilian life. For much of the war, such prejudice kept black soldiers from getting the promotions, respect, and pay that white soldiers received.

When the Civil War started, Isabelle was a lieutenant in the First Louisiana Native Guards, a militia company composed of free black men from New Orleans. (A fair number of the more than 180,000 free blacks in the South lived in New Orleans. Blacks of French and Spanish heritage were guaranteed freedom when France gave the Louisiana Territory to the United States.)

Similar militia groups had been formed by state governments throughout the South to help the Confederate Army defend major cities. The Louisiana Native Guards never fought for the Confederacy, but when Yankee troops captured the city in the spring of 1862, Isabelle's company eagerly offered its services to the Union.

General Benjamin Butler, the Union commander, refused the offer at first, but later changed his mind and mustered the guards into the army. Butler also permitted the guards' officers—all of whom were black—to keep their rank.

Black Sailors

The Union Navy offered black men the opportunity to serve their country long before the army did. In fact, free blacks had never been barred from naval service, and former slaves were encouraged to enlist as early as September 1861, almost a year before they were admitted into the army.

The navy also treated black recruits better than the army did. They were paid the same as white sailors of equal rank; they performed the same duties, bunked in the same quarters, and ate at the same tables. The relative lack of discrimination resulted mainly from practical necessity. There simply was not enough room on the ships to house and feed the men separately. The navy was also chronically short of men and could not afford to lose black soldiers because of unfair treatment.

Black sailors served aboard every ship in the Union fleet. Some crews were almost entirely black. They manned the ships that blockaded Confederate ports, the ships that went up rivers to collect supplies and contrabands, the gunboats that fired on rebel forts, and the oceangoing vessels that protected northern merchant ships from Confederate raiders.

As many as twenty thousand black men served in the Union Navy. Many were former slaves who took immense risks to join up, swimming or rowing small boats out to Union ships anchored near their plantations. Some eight hundred black sailors were killed in battle; another two thousand died of disease. Black sailors also distinguished themselves in battle; eight won the U.S. Medal of Honor for extreme bravery.

Limited space aboard ship was one reason black and white sailors were not segregated as their army counterparts were.

The general who replaced Butler in December 1862, Nathaniel P. Banks, did not approve of blacks holding command positions and wanted to replace Isabelle and the Native Guards' black officers with white men. Since he could not legally strip the men of their

commissions, Banks set about making their lives so unbearable that they would resign voluntarily. He encouraged white soldiers to ridicule, defy, and snub the officers at every opportunity.

For weeks, Isabelle and other black officers endured the campaign of insults and humiliation. But one by one they lost heart and resigned their commissions. Isabelle held out longer than many of his fellow officers, but in March 1863 he, too, left the army. The lieutenant's hope that white soldiers would put aside prejudice "for the good of our country" had been crushed.

General Banks's view that black officers were "detrimental to the Service" was shared by most top War Department officials. No explicit policy existed, but everyone assumed that black regiments would be segregated from white units. By the same token, although no law prohibited the War Department from commissioning black officers, the assumption was that the men who led black units would all be white. No public official was willing to face the controversy that would erupt if black men were put in positions that would make them equal with, or even superior to, white officers.

Abolitionists, black leaders, and black soldiers, however, believed that qualified black men should have the same chance as white soldiers to advance through the ranks. But the War Department did not come around to this view until the war was nearly over. By then, through their outstanding performance and bravery on the battlefield, black soldiers had proved that they were, indeed, officer material. During the war's final months, ten black soldiers received commissions as officers.

With those few exceptions, however, black regiments were led by white officers. Many of those who volunteered to lead the first black regiments were abolitionists, men who had been pressing the federal government to ban slavery for years before the Civil War began. These officers were determined to see their black troops succeed, a commitment only strengthened by jibes from white men about "nigger officers"—the term applied to white officers who commanded black regiments.

Colonel Isaac F. Shepard, commander of the Third Missouri Colored Volunteers, was one white officer who demanded that his black troops be treated with respect. When a white soldier from another unit harassed his men, Shepard had the offender whipped, risking his career by doing so. Officers such as Colonel Thomas Wentworth Higginson of the First South Carolina Volunteers sought every opportunity to encourage their men's advancement, including setting up schools in camp to teach former slaves, most of whom were illiterate, to read and write.

Colonel Thomas J. Morgan, a Rhode Islander who organized and led several regiments of former slaves, recalled how enthusiastic his men were about reading lessons. Before long, Morgan said, the men who went on picket or guard duty took their books with them, considering them "as indispensable as their coffee pots."

But there were only so many abolitionists with the desire and experience to lead a military regiment. With more and more black volunteers enlisting every day, the Bureau of Colored Troops had to draw from a larger pool in recruiting white officers.

Each officer candidate was given a grueling oral test assessing his leadership ability and knowledge of military regulations and tactics. Unfortunately, the exams did not include any questions about

Illiterate black soldiers sought every chance to learn to read and write. In some units, missionaries distributed reading primers and taught classes.

the men's racial attitudes or why they were applying to serve in a black regiment.

If bureau examiners had asked such questions—and received honest answers—they might have screened out some of the most racist applicants. Instead, many prejudiced men, including a few slaveowners, were commissioned to lead black troops.

Motivated only by the quick route to a higher rank—and the good pay that went with it—many officers of black regiments felt contempt for their men and showed it openly. They humiliated their soldiers by forcing them to act as their personal servants and laughing at their ignorance. Some even took advantage of their soldiers' illiteracy by cheating them out of wages.

Most white officers, though, were neither racist monsters nor abolitionist saints, but were somewhere in between. Even the most open-minded officers believed in the common stereotypes of blacks as being childlike and less intelligent than whites. And a good number of the most prejudiced officers came to respect their troops as they saw them display courage as great as any white soldier's.

The only leadership experience most black soldiers got during the Civil War was as noncommissioned officers—corporals and sergeants. These men were chosen by their company commander and given a variety of responsibilities, including keeping records and ordering supplies. Noncommissioned

The Union Army set up recruiting stations throughout the North to find white officers to lead black troops.

officers also sometimes led small detachments on picket duty and on the battlefield.

Unlike commissioned officers, sergeants and corporals remained enlisted men and enjoyed no special privileges. They ate the same food as the rest of the troops, slept in the same barracks, shined their own boots, and cleaned their own guns. Still, noncommissioned officers did have the chance to develop writing and management skills that would serve them well after the war when they wanted to get started in a business, profession, or trade.

Officers or not, black soldiers were reminded daily that the government they were fighting for valued them less than white soldiers. They were routinely given spoiled food, defective guns and poorly made uniforms. White troops, too, occasionally received substandard equipment and rations, but not as a general practice.

A gulf also existed between the amount of training black and white troops received—although this was the result not just of discrimination but also of circumstance. Most white soldiers, who signed up early in the war, had trained for months in northern camps before being sent south. Most black soldiers, on the other hand, were recruited close to the scene of battle, at a time when the need for fresh troops was acute.

It was up to the officers of black regiments to teach their recruits the military commands, tactics, and maneuvers they would need to succeed on the battlefield. The best officers believed in their men's ability to make excellent soldiers and devoted every spare minute to training. When Colonel Thomas Wentworth Higginson took command of the First South Carolina Colored Volunteers in late 1862, many of the men had already been in battle, "but they were very ignorant of drill and camp duty," Higginson reported. Believing in the value of constant practice, the colonel spent hour after hour putting his men through their paces on fields set aside for drilling, holding target practice, and explaining guard duty. He was lucky enough to have nearly two months before his troops saw action again. Other officers had even less time, and were forced to take their troops into battle with little or no formal training.

Not all officers of black soldiers shared Higginson's faith in their men's abilities. Such officers devoted little time to drilling and were far less patient with their recruits. "They strike the men with their swords and jab and punch them in their side to show them how to drill," complained a private in the Forty-third U.S. Infantry.

When given even minimal training, most black soldiers quickly mastered the art of drilling, often surpassing the performance of white troops. "I have this afternoon taught my men to load-in-the-nine-times [load and fire guns]," one officer told Colonel Higginson, "and they do it better than we did it in my former [white] company in three months."

While some officers attributed black soldiers' aptitude for drilling to the fact that as former slaves they were used to obeying orders, others identified the real reason: Most black men regarded soldiering as an honor and privilege, and they worked hard at it.

Another constant reminder of army prejudice was the amount of military labor or "fatigue duty" assigned to black troops. While white soldiers rested in camp or marched off to battle, black soldiers toiled

Most, although not all, black soldiers from the North received basic training in drilling and other military exercises at Union camps before being sent to the battlefront. Camp Penn, outside Philadelphia, was one of the biggest training centers for black recruits.

Learning how to load and fire cannon quickly in battle required hours of practice in camp—hours that black soldiers were often denied because they were given so much fatigue duty.

eight to ten hours a day, every day except Sunday, digging trenches, building roads, loading and unloading supply wagons, and burying corpses. White officers justified this imbalance by saying they wanted to "save the white soldiers for fighting."

The unending work sapped the black soldiers' strength, health, and morale. Worst of all, it left them with no time to drill or practice other military exercises that would prepare them for battle. Not surprisingly, when the men were assembled for their weekly inspection, the black companies sometimes made a poor impression. Their uniforms were torn and shabby, their guns were dirty, and they looked haggard and unfit.

Black soldiers were saddled with most of the fatigue duty, including the gruesome task of burying the dead.

Rarely did inspecting officers attribute the men's condition to excessive fatigue duty. Usually, the soldiers' poor presentation strengthened the officers' belief that black soldiers were not fit for combat.

Black soldiers bitterly resented the unfair treatment. "Instead of the musket, it is the spade and the wheelbarrow and the axe," a private with a Louisiana regiment protested to President Lincoln. "Slavery with all its horrors can not [equal] this," another soldier declared, "for it is nothing but work from morning 'til night."

Private William G. Barcroft got so fed up one day that he threw down his shovel and announced he was not going to do another minute's worth of fatigue duty. He enlisted to be a soldier, not a laborer, he told his startled commanding officer. Complaining did no good. Barcroft was court-martialed for refusing to obey an officer and sentenced to two years of hard labor in a military prison.

The officers of black companies often joined their men in objecting to excessive fatigue duty. General Daniel Ullmann, in charge of several black regiments in Louisiana, turned for help to the U.S. Senate Committee on Military Affairs. Since he had been in command, Ullmann said, "such has been the amount of fatigue work thrust upon the organization that . . . months have passed, at times, without the possibility of any drill at all." The morale of his men, Ullmann reported, had plummeted "to an extent which I who command and come into constant contact with them daily deplore."

Hardest to bear for many black troops was being ordered to do white soldiers' work for them. Colonel James C. Beecher, commander of the Thirty-fifth U.S. Colored Infantry, griped repeatedly about the "incessant and trying" fatigue duty assigned to his unit. But when he learned that sixty of his men had been ordered to a nearby island to set up and police the camps of a white regiment from New York, Beecher was outraged.

"They have been slaves and are just learning to be men," the colonel wrote to his superior. "It is a draw-back that they are regarded as, and called 'd——d niggers' by so-called 'gentlemen' in uniform of U.S. Officers," Beecher said, "but when they are set to menial work doing for white regiments what those regiments are entitled to do for themselves, it simply throws them back where they were before and reduces them to the position of slaves again."

By June 1864, the flood of protests prompted the War Department to step in. The department issued an order forbidding camp commanders to assign more fatigue duty to black soldiers than to white. Although the order marked an important reform, it was hard to enforce.

Of all the injustices experienced by black soldiers during the Civil War none stung more sharply than the issue of unequal pay. Though they did the same work and ran the same risks as white soldiers, black soldiers were paid much less. In 1863, the standard monthly salary for a white enlisted man was thirteen dollars, *plus* a three-dollar clothing allowance, for a total of sixteen dollars. White noncommissioned officers received up to twenty-one dollars a month, as well as three dollars for clothes.

In June of that year, the War Department decided that black soldiers, regardless of rank, would be paid only ten dollars a month. From that, three dollars would be *deducted* for clothing, for a total monthly wage of seven dollars. Thus, a white enlisted man, with his monthly pay of sixteen dollars, would earn more than twice as much as a black sergeant. A white sergeant would earn seventeen dollars a month more than his black counterpart.

As they learned of this inequity, black soldiers—in many cases joined by their officers—protested to senior officers, to the secretary of war and to President Lincoln. Their letters filled the editorial sections of black northern newspapers.

"Do we not fill the same ranks?" asked one soldier in a letter to the *Christian*

Black regiments were often relegated to the more menial duties in camp. Here, they weigh and hand out rations from the commissary.

Recorder. "Do we not take up the same length of ground in the grave-yard that others do? The ball does not miss the black man and strike the white nor the white and strike the black. . . . At that time there is no distinction made."

A corporal in the Fifty-fourth Massachusetts, James Henry Gooding, put the matter plainly in a letter to President Lincoln: "Your Excellency, we have done a Soldier's Duty. Why Can't we have a Soldier's pay?"

When their protests failed to produce results, several regiments took direct action: They refused to accept *any* pay until their salary was raised to the same level as white soldiers. Among the first black units to take this position were the Fifty-fourth and Fifty-fifth from Massachusetts.

The men of the Fifty-fourth had been in the army for five months when their first payday arrived in August 1863. When called to attention, they lined up eagerly. Eagerness turned to disbelief and then anger when, instead of the thirteen dollars they had been promised by Governor John A. Andrew upon enlisting, the paymaster offered them only ten dollars—three of which they would never even see because of the clothing deduction.

Corporal Gooding described what happened next in one of his regular letters to the editor of the New Bedford *Mercury*, a newspaper in his Massachusetts hometown. "I am glad to say," wrote Gooding, "that when the officer in charge asked those who wished to receive the ten dollars to raise their right hands, not one man in the whole regiment lifted a hand."

The officer warned the troops that it might be months before they were paid again, Gooding reported. The men replied that they had been "over five months waiting," and would continue to wait until "the Government could frame some special law for the payment of part of its troops" before accepting less than what was owed them.

Twice more during the next few months the men of the Fifty-fourth and Fifty-fifth were "mustered in" for pay. Both times they were offered ten dollars and both times the men said no. Then Governor Andrew informed the troops that the Massachusetts Legislature had voted to supply the extra three dollars to make sure the troops received the same pay as white soldiers.

Private Theodore Tilton and other soldiers were offended by the governor's offer. In a letter to the *Boston Journal*, Tilton wrote that by his actions the governor "advertises us to the world as holding out for *money* and not from *principle*—that we sink our manhood in consideration for a few more dollars. . . . What false friend has

Discipline and Punishment

The black soldiers of the Fourth Louisiana Native Guards hated their bad-tempered colonel, Augustus W. Benedict, who for months had been "kicking and knocking men about." But when the troops saw the colonel whipping two drummer boys for a minor offense, they snapped.

Up to half the regiment stormed onto the parade ground and repeatedly fired their guns into the air to protest Benedict's actions. "[We] did not come here to be whipped by him," the men shouted. After half an hour, the men's white officers managed to convince them to stop shooting and return to their quarters. No one was hurt, but eight enlisted men were court-martialed.

For the most part, black soldiers, like white troops, accepted discipline and punishment as unavoidable aspects of military life. They recognized that no regiment could function in the chaos of battle unless troops could be counted on to obey their officers and work together as a team. A private in a black regiment contrasted army discipline with the unpredictability and cruelty of punishment in slavery: "Here if we are punished, we know why, for the officers tell us our duty and never punish us unless we disobey." Knowing that white troops were subject to the same rules and punishments as they were also made accepting discipline easier for black soldiers.

But some officers used a heavy hand with their black troops, kicking, cuffing, or whipping them, even though the army banned physical punishment. White enlisted men, too, were occasionally subjected to brutal treatment by officers, but black soldiers found punishment of this sort especially hard to tolerate. Former slaves were deeply sensitive to punishments that involved humiliation or physical abuse such as flogging or being been misrepresenting us to the Governor, to make him think that our necessities outweigh our self-respect?"

The officers of the two Massachusetts regiments fully supported the stand their men were taking. "They will refuse to accept any money from the United States until the United States is willing to

Above: **Soldiers who committed minor offenses were sentenced to "ride" the wooden horse.**

Left: **Benjamin Ditcher of the Fifty-fifth Massachusetts, who stole from a wounded friend, was sentenced to have his head shaved, his hands tied behind his back, and wear a large sign labeling him as a thief. To add to his shame, the culprit was forced to parade through camp, marching to the music of a fife and drum.**

forced to march through camp wearing a placard that broadcast their offense. Such treatment reminded them too much of slavery and the soldiers protested it loudly.

The best officers were sensitive to their men's feelings. They never punished them without due cause and avoided discipline that smacked of bondage. "Men will not obey, as promptly, an officer who adopts the customs of the slave driver to maintain authority," said the commander of a black Missouri regiment in criticizing his company officers for abusive treatment. Colonel Thomas Wentworth Higginson of the First South Carolina Colored Volunteers agreed: "Experience proved . . . [that] the more strongly we marked the difference between the slave and the soldier, the better for the regiment."

White officers who ignored these lessons paid the price. Augustus Benedict, for example, was drummed out of the service. Most instances of mutiny among black troops occurred in regiments whose commanders were brutal disciplinarians.

pay them according to the terms of their enlistment," said Colonel E. N. Hallowell of the Fifty-fifth in a letter to Governor Andrew explaining and defending his troops' actions. "They would rather work and fight until they are mustered out of the Service, without any pay, than accept from the Government less than it gives to other soldiers from Massachusetts."

The Fifty-fourth and Fifty-fifth were not the only northern black units that refused to settle for anything less than full pay. A regiment from Michigan and another from Rhode Island took the same stand. (Some two dozen members of the Fourteenth Rhode Island Heavy Artillery were court-martialed and sentenced to one year at hard labor for refusing to accept their pay. One enlisted man who violently objected to the sentence was shot and killed by a white lieutenant.)

Army life was not all drilling, fatigue duty, and fighting. Soldiers found time to organize regimental bands, which played at parades and other special occasions.

Nor were the black soldiers from the North the only ones who staged protests over unequal pay. At least one-third of the men of the First South Carolina Colored Volunteers also rejected the lower wages. Former slaves mustered into the army in late 1862 and early 1863, these soldiers had been assured by the War Department that they would receive the same pay as whites. In fact, they had received a full paycheck—thirteen dollars, plus the three-dollar clothing allowance—before the War Department slashed black soldiers' pay.

The men of the Third South Carolina Colored Volunteers took their protest over unfair pay a bold, but ill-fated, step further. Led by Sergeant William Walker, a noncommissioned officer, the company marched to the tent of its commander, Lieutenant Colonel Augustus G. Bennett. As he watched the men defiantly stack their rifles and ammunition belts in front of his tent, Bennett asked, "What does all this mean?" Walker told him that he and his men were "not willing to be soldiers for seven dollars per month."

Bennett warned the men that their actions constituted mutiny; he advised them to pick up their arms and return quietly to their quarters. The men refused. Sergeant Walker was court-martialed for leading a mutiny and shot by a firing squad in front of his entire brigade—more than two thousand soldiers.

While black soldiers stood firm on their refusal to accept unequal pay, their families suffered. Most black families were poor. They depended upon the money the men had expected to earn in the army. Every day, soldiers received heart-rending letters from their wives and relatives describing their poverty and hardship. Some families were reduced to living in poorhouses. Rachel Ann Wicker, wife of a black soldier from Ohio who was in the Fifty-fifth Massachusetts, wrote to Governor Andrew to find out why her husband had not been paid in fifteen months.

"I speak for my self and Mother and i know of a great many others as well as ourselve are suffering for the want of money to live on when provision and Clotheing wer Cheap we might have got a long But Every thing now is [triple] and over what it was some thre[e] year Back."

The soldiers worried constantly about the plight of their families, but they felt that they had to continue their protest until the policy was changed. Otherwise, their sacrifice would have meant nothing. The men of the Fifty-fourth and Fifty-fifth Massachusetts went for more than a year without wages. Not until August 1864, when Congress finally passed a law equalizing the pay of black and white soldiers, did the two regiments accept their pay. Reaching out to take the sixteen dollars (wages for privates had risen by then), the men shouted in celebration of their victory.

No one was celebrating in the nearby camp of the First South Carolina Colored Volunteers. Although under the new law they, too,

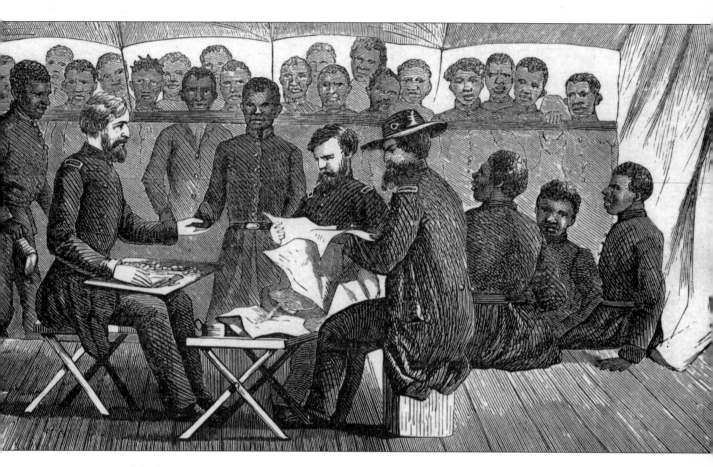

Black troops eagerly await their turn to receive their first full paycheck, after years of being paid less than white soldiers.

would begin receiving equal wages, the men learned they would not get all of the back pay to which they were entitled. The law stated that only men who were free when the war began would receive the pay allowed by law at the time they enlisted, and the members of the South Carolina regiment had been slaves. The troops vowed to continue without any wages until this discrimination, too, was corrected. Members of the First South Carolina Colored Volunteers continued their protest until March 1865—only a month before the end of the war—when Congress passed a second law allowing the higher pay for former slaves.

Though it was not against the enemy in the South, black soldiers had won one of the longest and most important battles of the Civil War—the fight for equal pay.

Soldiers raise their guns and caps in triumph as they haul their prize—a captured rebel cannon—back to camp.

FOUR

The Test of Battle

◆ ◆ ◆

After months of digging trenches, building fortifications, and repairing bridges, the First and Third Louisiana Native Guards were going into battle! The goal of the two black regiments was to capture Port Hudson, Louisiana, the southernmost Confederate stronghold on the Mississippi River. For both sides, the Mississippi was a vital route for moving men and supplies. Victory at Port Hudson would give the Union control of nearly all six hundred miles of the great waterway that flowed through the Confederacy.

Taking Port Hudson would not be easy. White Union troops had been trying to break through the rebel defenses since six o'clock that morning of May 27, 1863, with little result. The Confederates had built their main fortification on a bluff eighty feet above the river. The earthen walls of the fort were twenty feet thick and cannon were placed at intervals all along the fort's perimeter. Below the parapet were rifle pits in which sharpshooters waited to blast any Yankee who came within range. At the base of the bluff was a water-filled ditch.

As the white troops charged the bluff again and again, the two black regiments waited for their orders in a grove of willow trees, hidden from enemy view. The Louisiana units had been assembled

An artillery division of a black Louisiana regiment, their living quarters in the background, practice gun drills in preparation for the upcoming attack on Port Hudson.

in the worst possible position from which to make an assault. Between them and the bluff was a half mile of ground riddled with gullies and ravines and strewn with fallen trees and thick, tangled brush.

Looking at the dangers ahead, the men of the Louisiana Native Guards were scared. But they were also determined. This was their chance to prove themselves equal to whites—as soldiers and men.

At 10:00 A.M. the order came. Charge! The troops sprang forward, moving as quickly as they could over the rough terrain. As soon as the Native Guards cleared the trees, the Confederates opened fire with everything they had. Men fell by the dozens under a hail of bullets and artillery shells. Smoke from the cannon, mixed with dust stirred up by the men's feet, created a choking, blinding haze.

The noise of the guns was deafening. Trees knocked down by rebel shells fell on the troops, burying men under their branches.

The men of the Louisiana Native Guards pushed on. Just a few more yards and they would be close enough to return fire. But as they reached the base of the bluff, they were stopped by a moat—eight feet deep and twenty feet wide—formed by backwash from the Mississippi.

The troops were ordered to withdraw, but only temporarily. Again and again the men of the two Louisiana regiments regrouped and charged, each time suffering more casualties. Some soldiers plunged into the water, holding their rifles above their heads, in a futile attempt to ford the moat. Rebel soldiers picked them off easily.

The attack was called off late in the afternoon. Union forces were

Should We Arm Our Slaves?

Well before the North began arming black men in late 1862, calls had gone out in the South to do the same. The Confederate Army was losing thousands of men to death, disease, and desertion, and enlistment had fallen sharply. Couldn't slaves replenish the forces?

The majority of southern citizens said no. The idea of arming slaves ran counter to everything they believed. It was one thing to use them as laborers and servants for the Confederate troops, which the army had been doing since the war began, but quite another to employ them as soldiers. Opponents of slave enlistment insisted that black men were not fit to be soldiers—and that white troops would balk if told to fight alongside them. The controversy flared each time the Confederacy suffered a major defeat.

It was not until November 1864, with the rebels' military prospects looking grim, that Confederate President Jefferson Davis finally threw his support behind black enlistment; still, Congress hesitated. The war was nearly over when a "Negro Soldiers Law" approving black enlistment was passed in March 1865.

Efforts to recruit black soldiers were limited and few slaves signed up. One man, asked whether he would shoot at Yankees if the Confederates put a musket in his hand, expressed the view of thousands of slaves: "I nebber will shoot de Yankees; de first chance I git I run away."

no closer to breaking through Confederate defenses than they had been that morning, and the cost in men was too high to continue. Nearly two hundred black soldiers had been killed or wounded.

In a military sense, the assault on Port Hudson was a failure. But in showing the mettle of black soldiers, it was a spectacular success. In their first major test of the war, black troops had displayed great bravery and coolness under fire.

"You have no idea how my prejudices with regard to Negro troops have been dispelled by the battle the other day," wrote a white officer who witnessed the assault. "The brigade of Negroes behaved magnificently and fought splendidly."

Port Hudson "settles the question that the Negro race can fight," proclaimed the *New York Times*, which had been among the doubters. "Those black soldiers had never before been in any severe engagement and were yet subjected to the most awful ordeal that even veterans ever have to experience. . . . The men, white or black, who will not flinch from that will flinch from nothing."

Ten days later and 120 miles away, black soldiers had a second

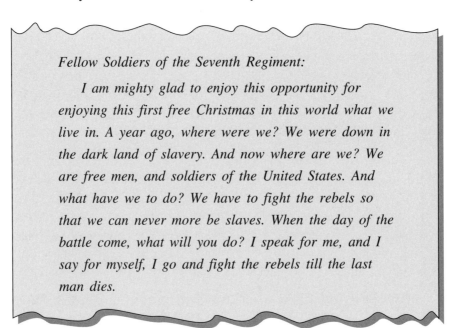

Fellow Soldiers of the Seventh Regiment:

I am mighty glad to enjoy this opportunity for enjoying this first free Christmas in this world what we live in. A year ago, where were we? We were down in the dark land of slavery. And now where are we? We are free men, and soldiers of the United States. And what have we to do? We have to fight the rebels so that we can never more be slaves. When the day of the battle come, what will you do? I speak for me, and I say for myself, I go and fight the rebels till the last man dies.

Soldiers grew more homesick than ever during the holidays, but black soldiers found reason to celebrate their first Christmas in the army. A member of the Seventh Louisiana Regiment Corps D'Afrique boosted his regiment's spirits with this speech in December 1863.

chance to prove themselves, this time by defending a federal post against a sudden Confederate attack. The 1,250 black soldiers who made up most of the Union force stationed at Milliken's Bend, Louisiana, were former slaves who had been in the army for just two weeks. They had received virtually no training and had been saddled with worn-out, barely functioning rifles.

Nevertheless, when surprised by a Confederate attack in the middle of the night on June 7, the black troops responded like seasoned soldiers. As the rebels ran forward over open fields toward the Union post, they were met by a volley of musket fire. The rebels slowed for a moment, but when no second round came, they pressed ahead.

"No quarter!" the rebels yelled (meaning "no mercy, even if they surrender") as they swarmed over the breastworks surrounding the post.

Before the black troops could reload their troublesome rifles, the rebels were upon them. For the rest of the night and throughout the morning, the two sides engaged in fierce hand-to-hand combat, using their bayonets and rifle butts. Relief came at noon, after nine hours of fighting, when the Union gunboat *Choctaw* arrived and her crew opened fire on the rebels outside the post. Exhausted and dehydrated from fighting in the hundred-degree heat, the rebels pulled back.

Union soldiers, just as tired but buoyed by triumph, pursued the retreating troops, taking several prisoners. "One brave man took his former master prisoner," an eyewitness reported, "and brought him into camp with great gusto."

The fighting over, the Union troops and their officers surveyed the battlefield; it was a gruesome sight. Mangled and bloody bodies littered the ground. One observer reported that "white and black men were lying side by side, pierced by bayonets, and in some instances transfixed to the earth. In one instance, two men, one white and the other black, were found dead, side by side, each having the other's bayonet through his body."

The captain of one black regiment, who had fought in some of the Civil War's bloodiest battles, declared Milliken's Bend "a horrible fight, the worst I was ever engaged in."

The black regiments sustained enormous losses: 101 killed, 285 wounded, and 264 captured or missing. Nearly half of the 300 men of the Ninth Louisiana Infantry of African Descent were killed or

Most of the fighting at the Battle of Milliken's Bend, Louisiana, was hand-to-hand using bayonets—the detachable steel blade stuck in the muzzle end of a rifle. Bayonets were not widely used during the Civil War because, as one general observed, "one of the party [usually] gives up before coming into contact with steel."

wounded—the highest casualty rate suffered by any black or white unit in a single day during the Civil War.

As at Port Hudson, the performance of black soldiers at Milliken's Bend won high praise from army officials. "I never saw a braver company of men in my life," remarked their white captain. "Not one of them offered to leave his place until ordered to fall back. . . . They met death coolly, bravely." Declared the captain, "I never more wish to hear the expression 'the niggers won't fight.'"

Even white soldiers who resented having to fight alongside blacks were impressed. "I never believed in niggers before," a Wisconsin cavalry officer admitted, "but by Jasus, they are hell in fighting."

No other Civil War battle in which black soldiers fought did more to establish their bravery than the assault on Fort Wagner in July 1863. Located on the northern end of Morris Island in South Carolina, Fort Wagner protected the entrance to Charleston harbor. Capturing the fort would allow the Union to cut off one of the Confederacy's main supply routes.

But could an assault on Fort Wagner possibly succeed? Protected on three sides by natural barriers, the fort could be approached only from the south along a narrow strip of beach. Any Union soldier lucky enough to survive the half-mile dash up the beach without being mowed down by rebel artillery would still have to cross a waist-deep moat and clamber up a twenty-five-foot-high, man-made mountain of sand and logs before reaching the enemy.

Union officials decided that the prize was worth the risk and set the attack for July 18. Union artillery and gunboats would bombard the fort all day to weaken its defenses and then, at sunset, the infantry would be sent in to finish the job.

When orders came through to report immediately to Morris Island, the black soldiers of the Fifty-fourth Massachusetts had just come under fire for the first time, beating the rebels in a fight for control of nearby James Island.

It was pitch dark and pouring rain when the regiment set out for the other side of James Island, where they would be met by a transport ship that would take them to Folly Island, the next stop on their route to Fort Wagner. They trudged wearily along a narrow, muddy path, their heads down to shield their faces from the strong winds and pelting rain.

When the men of the Fifty-fourth reached the rendezvous point, it was still raining, and the transport ship had not arrived. Grateful for the chance to rest, the men collapsed on the white, sandy beach.

The ship appeared at dusk. Since there was no dock from which to board, it took hours to ferry the soldiers from the shore to the transport in a leaky longboat that could carry only thirty men at a time. When the ship set them ashore on Folly Island, it was mid-morning, brutally hot, and the men faced a punishing six-mile march across the island to the spot where they would wait for another transport to take them to Morris Island.

By the time the Fifty-fourth reached the headquarters of General George C. Strong, it was nearly six o'clock in the evening. The men were exhausted and hungry, having gone more than two days without food or sleep. But they barely had time to catch their breath before they were ordered to assemble for the assault on Wagner. The Fifty-fourth would lead the charge!

The troops saw this as an honor, but it was not intended as one. In deciding on a battle strategy, the general in charge, Truman Seymour, had told other officers: "I guess we will let Strong lead and put those d——d niggers from Massachusetts in the advance; we may as well get rid of them, one time as another."

When General Strong gave the signal, the soldiers of the Fifty-fourth cast off their exhaustion and hunger. "Forward, Fifty-fourth!" yelled their young colonel, Robert Gould Shaw. Inspired by his call, they pushed to within a few hundred feet of the fort. There, the beach narrowed to less than one hundred feet and the men had to break formation to get through. As the troops slowed and began moving through the opening, rebel artillery and musket fire seemed to burst on them from every direction.

Scores of men at the front of the line fell, but those behind charged on "with set jaws, panting breath, and bowed heads." They plunged into the shallow ditch that separated them from the fort and began scrambling up the high earthen wall toward the rebel fortifications. "The rebel fire grew hotter . . . and a field piece every few seconds seemed to sweep along our rapidly thinning ranks," a black sergeant said later. "Men all around me would fall and roll down the scarp into the ditch."

The air was filled with exploding hand grenades, musket fire, and grapeshot. "I had my sword-sheath blown away while on the parapet of the Fort," Lewis Douglass wrote to his father in a quiet moment after the battle. "Swept down like chaff, still our men went on and on."

Despite the ferocity of the Confederate fire and the by-now complete darkness, Shaw and some of his men managed to reach the top of the wall from which the rebel troops were shooting. For a few moments they fought the enemy hand-to-hand with their bayonets and rifle butts.

"Rally! Rally!" Shaw shouted to his men, waving his sword. Seconds later, the valiant colonel was struck down by a rebel bullet. The regiment's flag bearer fell along with Shaw. But before the colors could touch the ground, William H. Carney of Company C managed to grab it.

Even the great bravery of the Fifty-fourth could not overcome the formidable rebel defenses. The Massachusetts regiment was hopelessly outnumbered and the white units that were supposed to reinforce the Fifty-fourth moved too slowly to take advantage of the black troops' initial attack. The regiment was forced to pull back. That, too, was dangerous. "The line of retreat seemed lit with infernal fire," said one soldier. "The hissing bullets and bursting shells seemed angry demons."

The Fifty-fourth lost 247 men in the attempt to take Fort Wagner, more than any of the other ten regiments participating in the attack. Among the survivors was twenty-two-year-old William Carney, who, despite being wounded in the head, chest, right arm, and leg, crawled back into camp still holding the company colors.

Another survivor was James Henry Gooding, who later described the battle for the readers of the New Bedford *Mercury*. (Gooding was taken prisoner after the Battle of Olustee, Florida, in February 1864; he died five months later in a Confederate prison camp.) Both Carney and Gooding received medals of honor for their valor at Fort Wagner.

The rebels buried Colonel Shaw with his men in a mass grave, intending to insult the Union Army. Typical military practice was to bury officers separately, but the fact that the colonel and the men of the Fifty-fourth shared a common grave became a source of pride to black soldiers. When Shaw's father learned that Union officials were trying to recover his son's body, he insisted that it remain in the grave with his men: "We hold that a soldier's most appropriate burial place is on the field where he has fallen."

The stories of black soldiers' heroics at Port Hudson, Milliken's Bend, and Fort Wagner silenced the critics who had predicted that

The charge of the Fifty-fourth Massachusetts at Fort Wagner has been depicted more often than any other battle scene involving black soldiers in the Civil War. Here, Colonel Robert Gould Shaw is shown rallying his men as a rebel bullet strikes him.

black men either would not, or could not, fight. Black civilians felt immense pride when they heard of the soldiers' performance, and enlistment shot up throughout the North.

New black enlistees could not count on having such dramatic opportunities to show their courage and ability. Most black troops continued to serve behind the battle lines. When Port Hudson fell to the Yankees in July 1863, for example, the Union had more than six hundred miles of the Mississippi to oversee and protect. Much of this work fell to black soldiers. They manned fortifications along the river, guarded plantations and contraband camps, and arranged for the transportation of supplies and equipment.

Tens of thousands of black soldiers also worked behind the scenes to make possible General William Tecumseh Sherman's famous march through Georgia. During the second half of 1864, Sherman led his armies from Atlanta to the Atlantic Ocean, destroying everything in his path in an effort to "break the spirit of the Confederacy." The general did not think black soldiers were qualified to be in the front line of his advancing forces. Instead, he used them to keep his white troops supplied, to protect troops at the rear of the march from attack, and to lift wagons and cannon out of mudholes. Black soldiers also built the bridges and corduroy roads—made by laying logs side-by-side across muddy ground—that allowed wagons and troops to pass safely and quickly over water and rugged terrain.

Fort Pillow Massacre

Even war has rules. But when it came to the treatment of black soldiers captured in battle, the Confederates refused to play by them.

Ground rules, agreed to by both the North and South, stated that captured soldiers were to be held as prisoners of war until they were exchanged or the war ended. Then they were to be released. But the Confederates did not consider black men—even free black men—to be real soldiers. They considered them fugitive slaves. The officers who led these men were criminals, too, Confederates believed, and their crime should be punished severely.

Jefferson Davis, president of the Confederate States of America, told his generals that captured officers of black regiments were to be put "to death or be otherwise punished at the discretion" of a military court. Their men were to be turned over to authorities in the state where they were captured "to be dealt with according to the present or future law of such State or States." For most black soldiers that meant death by hanging or being returned to slavery.

Just how black prisoners were treated depended on the commander who captured them. Most Confederate officers either returned black soldiers to their masters, sold them into slavery, or put them to work doing military labor.

There were also cases where black soldiers were killed after they had surrendered. The worst such case became known as the Fort Pillow Massacre.

On the morning of April 12, 1864, fifteen hundred Confederate troops under the

Ignoring the rules of war, Confederate General Nathan Bedford Forrest and his troops slaughtered as many as three hundred unarmed black soldiers.

command of Confederate General Nathan Bedford Forrest attacked the Union garrison at Fort Pillow, Tennessee, on the Mississippi River. The fort was defended by 570 Union soldiers, almost half of them black. The Yankees had just beat back a second assault when, suddenly, the enemy stopped firing. A small group of rebel soldiers approached the fort waving a white flag. They carried a letter from General Forrest demanding that the Union troops surrender and promising that all who did would be treated as prisoners of war.

The Union commander refused to yield and the rebels stormed the fort again, this time breaking through its defenses and taking control.

The defeated soldiers threw down their guns and surrendered. According to the rules of war, all fighting should have stopped right then. But it did not. Eyewitnesses reported that rebel soldiers opened fire on the now defenseless Union troops. "Until dark and at intervals throughout the night, our men were shot down without mercy and almost without regard to color," said one survivor. "The horrid work of butchery began again next morning."

It is impossible to say exactly how many Union soldiers were murdered at Fort Pillow. A federal investigation estimated that three hundred men had been massacred, although this report was later shown to be exaggerated.

The atrocities of the Fort Pillow Massacre were reported throughout the North. The news sparked a public outcry, especially among black Americans, who demanded that the government do more to protect captured black soldiers.

President Lincoln, too, was appalled by the accounts of murder and enslavement of captured black soldiers. In July 1863, he had issued an order stating that "for every soldier of the United States killed in violation of the laws of war a rebel soldier shall be executed, and for every one enslaved by the enemy or sold into slavery a rebel soldier shall be placed at hard labor on the public works."

Unfortunately, his policy proved nearly impossible to enforce. Black citizens continued to feel betrayed by a government that, as they saw it, could not take adequate steps to protect black prisoners of war.

For black soldiers, the knowledge that capture might mean slavery or death only made them fight harder. "Remember Fort Pillow" became a rallying cry for black soldiers everywhere.

THE MASSACRE AT FORT PILLOW

Official Confirmation of the Report.

Three Hundred Black Soldiers Murdered After Surrender.

Fifty-three White Soldiers Killed and One Hundred Wounded.

RETALIATION TO BE MADE

News of the Fort Pillow Massacre made headlines throughout the North.

If black troops had far fewer chances than white soldiers to meet the enemy in battle, they still saw action in every state where fighting occurred, distinguishing themselves in nearly every case.

In late December 1864, at the Battle of Nashville, black troops played a decisive role in turning back a rebel offensive that might

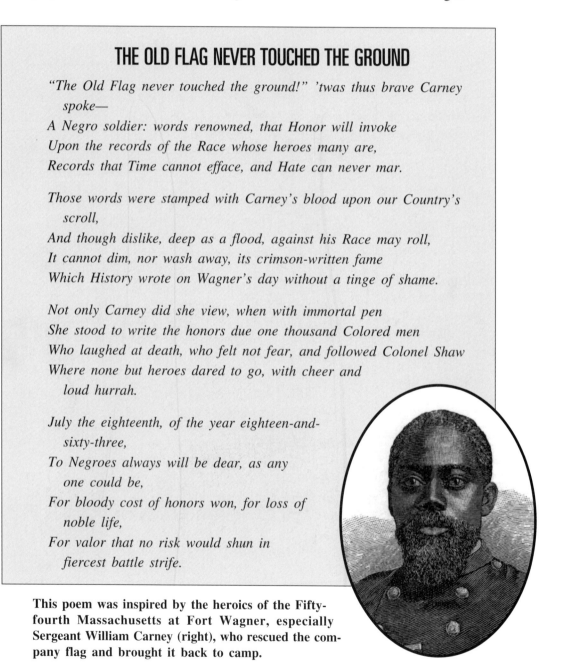

THE OLD FLAG NEVER TOUCHED THE GROUND

*"The Old Flag never touched the ground!" 'twas thus brave Carney
   spoke—*
A Negro soldier: words renowned, that Honor will invoke
Upon the records of the Race whose heroes many are,
Records that Time cannot efface, and Hate can never mar.

*Those words were stamped with Carney's blood upon our Country's
   scroll,*
And though dislike, deep as a flood, against his Race may roll,
It cannot dim, nor wash away, its crimson-written fame
Which History wrote on Wagner's day without a tinge of shame.

Not only Carney did she view, when with immortal pen
She stood to write the honors due one thousand Colored men
Who laughed at death, who felt not fear, and followed Colonel Shaw
*Where none but heroes dared to go, with cheer and
   loud hurrah.*

*July the eighteenth, of the year eighteen-and-
   sixty-three,*
*To Negroes always will be dear, as any
   one could be,*
*For bloody cost of honors won, for loss of
   noble life,*
*For valor that no risk would shun in
   fiercest battle strife.*

This poem was inspired by the heroics of the Fifty-fourth Massachusetts at Fort Wagner, especially Sergeant William Carney (right), who rescued the company flag and brought it back to camp.

have forced Sherman to abandon his march through Georgia and come to the aid of Union forces in Tennessee.

The Union strategy was to trick the Confederate commander, General John Bell Hood, into thinking that they would concentrate their attack on his right. The Union leadership was betting that Hood would react by pulling troops away from his left to fend off the onslaught on his right, creating an opening for the Yankees to smash through the rebel lines.

Scouts played a critical role in the Union Army, traveling ahead of the troops into enemy territory to obtain information on rebel activities. Former slaves who had enlisted close to home made especially good scouts because they were familiar with the countryside.

For much of the ten months it took the Union to capture Petersburg, Virginia, these and other black soldiers lived alarmingly close to enemy lines in shallow "bombproofs." Their job was to keep the troops in the trenches behind them informed of Confederate troop movements.

The deception worked perfectly, in large part thanks to the four black regiments who were among the units attacking on the right.

At the end of the first day of the two-day battle, Colonel Thomas J. Morgan, the commander of the black regiments, noted that "Colored soldiers had again fought side by side with white troops;

they had mingled together in the charge; they had supported each other; they had assisted each other from the field when wounded, and they lay side by side in death. The survivors rejoiced together over a hard fought field, won by a common valor."

One of the most spectacular, if disastrous and bloody, battles in which black soldiers fought was the Battle of the Crater in Petersburg, Virginia, in July 1864. By then, both the Union and the Confederate armies had concentrated most of their forces in Virginia. For months, both sides sought control of two key cities: Richmond, the capital of the Confederacy, and Petersburg, a major railroad center used to move rebel soldiers and supplies.

Aside from occasional skirmishes that neither side seemed to win, there was little action. Yankees and rebels alike spent most of their time crouched uncomfortably in narrow trenches or hiding behind dirt barricades.

Frustrated by the seemingly endless standoff, Union commanders adopted a desperate ploy. They would blow up a rebel fort guarding Petersburg. Union troops, backed by artillery fire, would take advantage of the resulting chaos by storming through Confederate defenses on either side of the crater created by the blast and capturing the city. For two weeks, Union forces dug a tunnel to reach the rebel stronghold. Once underneath the fort, they built a mine containing 8,000 pounds of gunpowder in 320 wooden barrels—powerful enough to blow up several forts.

The soldiers of the Colored Division of the Ninth Army Corps, comprising eight black regiments, had not seen action for several months. They were promised they could lead the assault. But Union officers changed their minds at the last minute and decided to send three white regiments in first.

The officers feared that if they allowed black troops to lead the attack, "and if it should prove a failure, it would be said only very properly, that we were shoving these people ahead to get killed because we did not care anything about them." In fact, black troops were far better prepared than the white soldiers who wound up in front; the black soldiers had been drilling continuously since work on the tunnel began.

Nothing went according to plan. The mine itself did not blow up until 4:50 A.M., more than an hour behind schedule. The explosion sent rebel soldiers, guns, sand, rock, and timber soaring two hundred feet into the air. Once the dust and smoke had cleared, the men saw that the fort was gone. In its place was a gigantic crater 30 feet deep, 60 feet wide, and 170 feet long.

The Union artillery immediately began firing heavy guns, and the first infantry regiment was ordered to advance. But as the men reached the edge of the crater, they stopped, transfixed by the sight of this great hole "filled with dust, great blocks of clay, guns, broken carriages, projecting timbers and men buried in various ways." The second and third regiments, which by then had been ordered to move, bumped up against the first. The men's commander yelled at them to move forward. But instead of circling to the left and right of the crater as planned, the Yankees went "jumping, sliding, and tumbling into the hole."

The rebel troops had recovered quickly and, safe in trenches or behind earthworks on either side of the crater, fired on any Union soldier who tried to follow the battle plan. The Confederates also brought cannon to the rim of the crater and began lobbing canisters at the men inside.

The white troops in the crater tried to regroup for an attack, but, as one Union officer reported, "the firing on the crater now was incessant and it was as heavy a fire of canister as was ever poured continuously upon a single objective. It was as utterly impracticable to re-form a brigade in that crater as it would be to marshal bees into line after upsetting the hive."

Union commanders should have called a halt as soon as they saw what a fiasco their battle plan had created. Instead, they ordered the black brigade forward. Thanks to their steady drilling, the black regiments performed better than the white troops. Many managed to stick to the edges of the crater and engage the rebels in hand-to-hand combat. (They took two hundred prisoners for the only victory of the day.) But hundreds of other black troops were forced by the Confederate fire into the crater, which by now was crammed with dead, dying, and wounded soldiers. Any man who tried to crawl up the steep sides to safety was gunned down by a rebel musket.

Casualties (dead and wounded) among the black brigade totaled 1,327—more than in any of the three white divisions in the battle. Later, it was discovered that the two generals "supposedly" in command of

Christian A. Fleetwood

Sergeant Major Christian Fleetwood was one of seventeen black soldiers to receive the U.S. Medal of Honor for extreme valor. During the Battle of Chaffin's Farm in Virginia in 1864 Fleetwood rescued the company colors after two flag bearers were shot down.

the Battle of the Crater, James H. Ledie and Edward Ferrero, spent the entire battle hiding in a bomb shelter.

By the time the Union won the Civil War in April 1865, black soldiers had fought on 449 different battlefields and had played an important role in 39 major engagements, including the Union's final assaults on the Confederacy. In several battles, their contributions made the difference between Union victory and loss. Eight hundred black sailors died at sea and some 3,000 black soldiers were killed on the battlefield. Another 35,000 black enlisted men lost their lives to wounds or disease. Seventeen black soldiers and eight sailors received the U.S. Medal of Honor for extreme valor.

By the end of the war, few Americans—in the North or South—questioned the nerve and prowess of black servicemen. Through their participation, these troops helped shorten the war and prevent even greater loss of life.

A proud mother makes final adjustments to her son's uniform as he pre-
pares to leave home to join his regiment.

FIVE

Defending Their Families

◆　　◆　　◆

P atsey Leach supported her husband, Julius, in his determination to join the Union Army and fight for freedom, even though it meant leaving her and their children behind in slavery. The couple had agreed that it was too dangerous for the entire family to try to escape from the Kentucky plantation where they lived. Instead, Julius would head for the nearest Union recruiting station and, once he had enlisted, find a way to free Patsey and the children.

Julius reached Union lines safely and joined the cavalry, but was killed in action at Salt Works, Virginia, less than a month later. Patsey was left to suffer the wrath of her master, Warren Wiley. Wiley was a bad-tempered man who blamed her for the loss of Julius—a valuable piece of property—and decided she would pay with the skin on her back.

After Julius died, Wiley beat Patsey more savagely than usual. One day, he tied her hands, tore the dress off her back, bent her forward until her head was between her knees, and whipped her until her "back was lacerated all over, the blood oozing out in several places . . . " He finally stopped, exhausted, but swore he would kill her the next day.

Patsey did not wait to see if Wiley would carry out his threat.

That night she took her youngest child—she knew she would never make it with all five—and ran to the local depot, where she caught a train for Lexington, Kentucky. From there she went to Camp Nelson, a federal post, and safety.

Like Patsey Leach, the relatives of black soldiers in the South took immense pride in the bravery of their husbands, fathers, and sons who escaped to fight for the Union. But their pride was mixed with anxiety over how they would manage with their chief bread-winners far away, possibly for years. Many slave families worried with good reason. Not only were women and children often forced to do the heavy labor usually reserved for men, but many were mistreated by vengeful masters. Some slaveowners whipped and terrorized soldiers' wives, and withheld food and clothing. The most

Wives, children and mothers say their last goodbyes as black recruits board a steamer that will take them to their regiment in South Carolina.

spiteful masters sold wives and children or sent them away to distant plantations where their husbands and fathers would never be able to find them.

In the North, black women whose husbands had gone to war felt the same pride as southern slave women. But they, too, found life difficult with their men away. Although they did not have to cope with abuse by slaveowners, they did have to worry about how they would pay for food, rent, and clothing.

Being free was no guarantee of a job or a livable wage, and many northern black families were desperately poor. Since few jobs available to black women paid enough to support a family, most women depended heavily on what money their husbands or sons sent them. Often this was not enough: Army pay was low to begin with, and lower still for black soldiers. Even worse, the troops sometimes went months without getting paid—usually the result of bureaucratic bungling—and they could not send any money to their families.

The situation grew so dire for some families that they were forced to leave their homes and move into the local poorhouse. In communities with no poorhouse or other charity, homeless families scraped by any way they could; some nearly starved to death.

The families of white soldiers, too, felt the bite of hunger when the men were not paid on time. But most white families were not as poor as black families. Also, white soldiers had received a single large payment, or "bounty," of as much as three hundred dollars when they enlisted. This money was often put aside for just such emergencies. Some black soldiers were promised bounties, too, but most didn't receive them until the war was over.

The relatives of black soldiers did everything they could to get help, including writing to Secretary of War Edwin Stanton and President Lincoln. Those who could not read or write relied on literate friends or sympathetic neighbors to write letters for them.

Jane Welcome, who described herself as old and "blossaming for the grave," wrote to President Lincoln asking him to release her son, Mart, from his service as a sergeant with a Pennsylvania regiment. Her husband and other son were dead, Mrs. Welcome told the president, leaving Mart as her only source of support. But he had not been paid and had already been wounded twice. Her request was forwarded to the U.S. Bureau of Colored Troops, which informed the old woman that her son was too important to the Union cause for the army to let him go.

Private John Turner from Detroit, Michigan, had better luck. After serving nine months in the army without pay, he asked to be

discharged from the army. "My family are sick and absolutely naked, having no clothes to wear," the private wrote in his request. "They are also threatened with being turned into the street."

Turner did not know when he wrote his letter that his wife had already died of dysentery in a hospital in Alexandria, Virginia. Recognizing his plight, the military discharged Turner to care for his three young children.

Whether they had enlisted from the South or the North, black soldiers worried constantly about their families and took whatever steps they could to ease their suffering. Some former slaves tried to use their newfound power as soldiers to rescue loved ones from slavery.

Before the war began, Spotswood Rice of Missouri offered to buy his children, Mary and Caroline, from their owner, Kitty Diggs, but she refused. After enlisting in the army, Rice told Diggs that he did not intend to allow his children to remain in slavery: "You call my children your property," he wrote, "not so with me, my Children is my own and I expect to get them."

A thousand black troops would be coming through her town soon, Rice warned the slaveholder, and when they did, he would get his children back. "When I get ready to come after [my children]," he told Diggs, "I will have . . . a

Black families in Beaufort, South Carolina, made money selling fruits, vegetables, and baked goods to soldiers.

power and authority to bring [them] away and to exacute vengencens on them that holds my Child[ren]."

At the same time, Rice wrote to Mary and Caroline to let them know that he would come for them. "Don't be uneasy my children. I expect to have you." Rice eventually succeeded in reuniting his family.

Sometimes, slaves who became soldiers sought the help of Union officers in freeing their families. Joseph J. Harris, a black sergeant

Staying in Touch

Like all soldiers away from home, black troops relied mainly on letters to keep in touch with their families and friends. But exchanging written correspondence was difficult for former slaves and their wives. Most could not read or write. Only family members lucky enough to have a literate friend or to know a local Union sympathizer could correspond. Their husbands, sons, and fathers had an easier time. Army chaplains and northern missionaries in the camps were usually willing to read and write letters for soldiers.

Even when writing or reading letters was not a problem for families left behind in slavery, receiving them was. Anything mailed directly to the plantation was sure to be intercepted by the slaveowner. If the letter contained money, the slaveowner might steal it. If it reported news of Union victories or other information the slaveowner did not want to hear, he might take out his anger on the sender's family. The only safe way to correspond was through a third party.

After searching for two weeks to find someone who would read letters sent by her husband, a Missouri slave named Ann Valentine was grateful when James Carney, a white, non-slaveholding neighbor, offered to read the letters and write back.

"They are treating me worse and worse every day," Ann told her husband through her correspondent. "Our child cries for you. Send me some money as soon as you can for me and my child are almost naked. . . . Do not send any of your letters to Hogsett [her owner] especially those having money in them as Hogsett will keep the money. Do the best you can and do not fret too much for me for it wont be long before I will be free and then all we make will be ours."

The note Carney included with Ann's letter revealed just how hard from Louisiana, was stationed in Florida when he learned that his parents and other enslaved relatives back home were being treated badly. Unable to leave his regiment, Harris wrote twice to ask General Daniel Ullmann, whose command included southern Louisiana, to rescue his family. In his letters, Harris told the general exactly how to reach the plantation and asked to be informed as soon as his family was safe, so he could send for them.

"Sir, it isn't more than 3 or 4 hours trouble," Harris told the

As soon as he joined a New York regiment, escaped slave John Boston wrote to his wife Elizabeth to tell her he was safe.

it was for slaves to send and receive mail. "Andy, if you send me any more letters for your wife do not send them in the care of any one. Just direct them plainly to James A Carney Paris Monroe County MO. Do not write too often. Once a month will be plenty and when you write do not write as though you had recd any letters for if you do your wife will not be so apt to get them. Hogsett has forbid her coming to my house so we cannot read them to her privately. If you send any money I will give that to her myself."

One way or another, over the course of the war, most black soldiers and family members found ways to share their news, their worries, and their love.

Dec 6 1865 Brazos Santiago Texas

W S C C Sir here is my
Compliment & wishes to be perfected
by the War Department

U S Colred Cavalry Sir Wee
present to you our Sufering
at present Concerning our
familys Wich Wee are now
informed that Commis derys has
been Closed a guinst them as
though Wee Were rebeling a guinst
U S and has came to be a great
Wonder & a great Condemplation
a mung the men of this regt
and wee would be hasfray
to find Some one to perfect
us in this Case wee have been
on dasley peldig from the Last
of fate up to this Day
without a furlough or any Comfort
what ever & our Wifes sends
letters stadeing thir suferage

Upon hearing that their families were suffering in their absence, men from
a black Virginia regiment offered to buy their way out of their remaining
army service so they could return home.

general. "I have bain trying evry sence I have bin in the servis, it is goin on ner 3 years & Could never get no one to so do for me."

Although some Union officers did help their men liberate family members, it is unlikely that General Ullmann would have gone so far out of his way for a soldier who was not even a member of a regiment under his command.

To protect them from abuses such as those suffered by Patsey Leach, some slaves took their families with them when they ran away to enlist. Many slaves who were recruited directly off plantations during Yankee raids agreed to join up only after being assured that their families could accompany them and would be fed and protected by the Union Army.

As a result, federal camps where black soldiers were stationed were often filled with their wives, children, and other relatives. Union camp commanders stationed in the Confederate states usually tolerated the presence of their men's families. The Emancipation Proclamation had declared slaves in rebellious states free, after all, and they could go where they liked.

Preoccupied with running their camps, however, even the most considerate officers did not give much thought to the welfare of the men's relatives, leaving them to fend for themselves. Consequently, life was hard for these families, especially during the cold winter months. Home was often no more than a cast-off army tent, an abandoned shed, or a flimsy shack built out of wood scraps and branches. The families used crude latrines, usually just holes in the ground. Women cooked in the open air, buying or bartering for food from sutlers—merchants who came into army camps to sell provisions.

For families who followed their husbands to Union lines, life was hard, with primitive shelters and scant supplies.

Escaped slaves who fled to Union lines went to great lengths to keep their families together.

Families got some aid from northern missionaries who distributed free blankets and clothing. The women and older children did whatever kind of work they could find, cooking, cleaning, doing laundry for the officers, and caring for wounded soldiers. Many worked as field hands on nearby plantations leased by northern farmers or owned by Southerners loyal to the Union.

For most black families, the comfort of being near their husbands and fathers outweighed the hardships of camp life.

Families could not count on being allowed to stay in camp, however, particularly if they were from the four border states. Under Union policy, slave men were considered free the moment they enlisted, but their families remained the property of their owners.

Union commanders who did not want their camps overrun by hundreds of extra people, many of them children, used this policy to drive black families out. Although they could not force the families to return to their owners (a practice that was prohibited in 1862), they could, and did, force them to leave the camp with instructions to "go home."

Some Yankee commanders in border state camps were kinder

and went out of their way to provide for the wives and children of their men. But even when they permitted black soldiers' wives and children to live in or near their camps, few Union officers in the Confederate or border states showed them much respect. Most did not consider them to be real families, because slaves had not been married in what white men considered a legal ceremony. What kind of a ceremony was "jumping over a broom," the common marriage ritual among slaves? officers asked themselves. Many considered their men's wives as little more than prostitutes.

One such officer was Colonel J. W. Lister, who supervised a Union camp in Bridgeport, Alabama, that was home to black regiments made up of former slaves. One of the enlisted men, George Buck Hanon, protested to Union officials that Lister kept his soldiers handcuffed, guarded them day and night, and refused to let them see their wives, some of whom had traveled as far as a hundred miles to reach the

Soldiers who were lucky enough to be stationed near home spent every free minute they could visiting with their families. Here, several families in Virginia pose for a picture.

camp. No such restrictions applied to commissioned officers, Hanon pointed out. "Every officer here that has a wife is got her here in camps," he said. "A colard man think jest as much of his wife as a white man dus of his," he protested, "but the way colonel luster is treating us it dont seem to me that he thinks we are human."

Lister expressed a bias shared by many white officers when he argued that "the marital relationship is but little understood by the colored race, and, if possible still less respected." In the eyes of black

Camp Nelson

Speed Fry, commander of the Union post at Camp Nelson, Kentucky, said he was tired of dealing with the "Nigger Woman Question." That is how he described the problem of caring for the wives who came to the camp to be near their soldier husbands or to escape brutal masters. During the war, Camp Nelson was temporary home to nearly ten thousand black soldiers and, at various times, hundreds of their relatives.

Fry, a slaveowner, did not want these women interfering with life at his camp. When soldiers' families refused to leave voluntarily, he evicted them by force and banned all runaway slaves from camp. When three women came back, Fry had them arrested, given "a few lashes," and sent away again. From then on, the camp commander warned, "Any negro woman here without authority will be arrested and sent beyond the lines and informed that, if they return, the lash awaits them."

Despite the threats, hardly a day passed in the summer without bringing "wives, children, and relatives into the camp," said Thomas Butler, a white missionary. Butler was one of a number of Camp Nelson residents who supported the right of soldiers' families to stay near them.

As many times as Fry ousted families with threats of arrest and punishment if they returned, they came back. For most of them, the alternatives waiting on the plantation were far worse than anything they might face at Camp Nelson.

Fry asked General Lorenzo Thomas, who oversaw the Bureau of Colored Troops, to support his decision. Thomas sided with the camp commander and issued an order requiring fugitive slave women and children to leave Union camps in border states. The general urged the women to return "home" where, "under the State laws, their masters are bound to take care of them."

Thomas worried about the cost to the federal government of caring soldiers, however, the bonds between black men and women were as enduring as those between white couples—and as deserving of respect.

Not all black families survived the Civil War intact. Thousands of women were widowed when enlisted men lost their lives; other marriages did not survive the long separation. But countless black families emerged from the war closer than they had been before. They also emerged intent on creating a new world of freedom and opportunity for their children.

for these families and he feared that the women might spread sexually transmitted diseases among the troops. The general was also more concerned about pleasing loyal slaveowners—who wanted their slaves back to work in the fields—than about the happiness of black soldiers and their families.

In an effort to settle the issue, Secretary of War Edwin Stanton ordered Fry to place the women and children in a protected camp away from the soldiers. Fry did as he was told, but in late November he again tried to force the families out. Giving them no time to gather their belongings or to prepare for the journey, Fry ordered all four hundred women and children living in the "protected" camp to leave immediately.

The families were loaded into wagons and carts, driven some distance from the camp and "dumped . . . in the streets or by the wayside in extremely cold weather." One observer reported seeing some of these women "lying in barns and mule sheds, wandering through the woods [and] languishing on the highway." Some froze to death.

Joseph Miller, a soldier who had come to Camp Nelson in mid-October with his wife and four children, blamed Fry for the death of his seven-year-old son. The boy was recovering from a serious illness the night a mounted guard gave Miller's wife "notice that she and her children must leave camp before early morning." When the soldier's wife protested that she had nowhere to go, the guard told her to get in the wagon or he would shoot her and her children. They left without even a chance to say good-bye.

After hours of searching, Joseph Miller found his family huddled in an old meeting house six miles from camp, hungry and shivering from the cold. His son was dead.

Stories of suffering and deaths caused by Fry's actions reached Secretary of War Stanton. He directed Camp Nelson's officers to provide food and shelter for all families of black soldiers who came into the camp from then on.

As the men of the Twenty-first and Fifty-fourth U.S. colored infantries march triumphantly through the streets of Charleston, South Carolina, black men, women, and children rejoice.

SIX

Victorious Freedmen

◆　　◆　　◆

In early 1865, the last Confederate strongholds began to fall. In February, the rebels abandoned Charleston, South Carolina; in late March, they left Petersburg and Richmond, Virginia. Black soldiers were honored and thrilled to be among the first Union troops to march into the conquered cities.

The men of the Twenty-first U.S. Colored Infantry led the march into Charleston, followed by a detachment from the Fifty-fourth Massachusetts. It was in Charleston that the war had begun four years earlier, and it was there that the men of the Fifty-fourth had fought so valiantly in the attempt to take Fort Wagner.

The few white citizens who had remained in Charleston kept out of sight. But black residents crowded the streets and windows, greeting the triumphant troops with "shouts, prayers, blessings, and songs." Men, women, and children rushed forward to shake the hands of black soldiers and their officers.

One old black woman grabbed the hands of a northern war correspondent and danced for joy. "I am sixty-nine years old, but I feel as if I wan't but sixteen," she said.

"Then you are glad the Yankees are here?" the reporter asked.

"O chile," the woman replied, "I doesn't call you 'Yankees.' I call you Jesus's aids, and I call you head man de Messiah."

Three months later, when Richmond fell, the black soldiers of the Fifth Massachusetts Cavalry were in the vanguard of the troops entering the Confederate capital. Within moments they were sur-

rounded by jubilant black men, women, and children. "Slavery chain done broke at last," sang the onlookers.

For black soldiers, especially those who had been slaves, the experience of marching through once-great southern cities, hailed as heroes and liberators, was profoundly moving. "The change seems almost miraculous," a black sergeant said. "The very people who, three years ago, crouched at their master's feet, on the accursed soil of Virginia, now march in a victorious column of freedmen, over the same land."

Another black soldier wrote from Wilmington, North Carolina, about the exhilaration of marching "through these fine thoroughfares where once the slave was forbid being out after 9:00 P.M. . . . or to walk with a cane, or to ride in a carriage! Negro soldiers—with banners floating."

For a private from the same regiment, the sight of "men and women, old and young . . . running through the streets, shouting and praising God," was ample reward for the risks and hardships he had endured. "We could then truly see what we had been fighting for," the soldier wrote.

On April 9, Confederate General Robert E. Lee surrendered to Union General Ulysses S. Grant at Appomattox, Virginia. The long, bloody war was over, but the duties of black soldiers were not. Most spent whatever remained of their military service on duty in the defeated South, helping to restore peace and stability. In cities and towns, they acted as military police, patrolling the streets and protecting freedmen and women. In rural areas, where many people

The happiest moment for a returning soldier was reuniting with his family.

had not yet heard about the Union victory, black soldiers delivered the news of freedom to tens of thousands of plantation slaves.

It was often black soldiers who gave the liberated slaves their first lessons in the rights and responsibilities of freedom. Soldiers helped former slaves understand what freedom meant, not only through their words, but also through their pride and self-confidence. Here were black men, most of them one-time slaves, who *expected* to be treated fairly by whites. When they were not, they protested to the authorities. This was a radical concept to people who had spent their entire lives as slaves.

Black soldiers also helped newly liberated slaves present their grievances to military and civil officials. In June 1865, E. S. Robison, a black sergeant stationed in Columbia, South Carolina, reported to the Union officer in charge of the region that a group of white men had broken into the home of Andrew Lee, a black man, "with a pretinse of searching for a hog that they Claimed to have lost." Lee had already complained to the commander of the local Union post, General Horton, who offered the former slave neither sympathy nor help. Horton told Lee that the white men had a right to search his house and that he ought to throw Lee in the guardhouse for complaining.

"Sir . . . in this I Could not hold my temper, after fighting to get wrights that White men might Respect By Virtue of the Law,"

Information wanted of Mrs. Nancy Massy. She was born and raised in Goochland County, VA. She was owned about fifteen years ago by John Michey. Her name before marriage was Nancy Brown. Anyone who can give any information in regard to her is requested to address,

Sergeant Olmstead Massy
76th USCT
via New Orleans

At the war's end, ads like this one placed by Sergeant Olmstead Massy began appearing in newspapers throughout the South as black soldiers tried desperately to find missing relatives. Massy had been sold away from his home in Virginia at age seventeen and was trying to find his long-lost mother.

One of the favorite duties of black soldiers who remained in the South after the war was liberating slaves whose masters had defied the Emancipation Proclamation.

Robison wrote to his commanding officer. In response to the sergeant's letter, his commander ordered an investigation, but no record of the outcome exists.

Calvin Holly, a black soldier posted to Vicksburg, Mississippi, informed a high government official that the local "colered people are in a great many ways being outraged beyond humanity" by white citizens. "Houses have been tourn down from over the heades of women and Children," wrote Holly. "The old Negroes after they have worked there till they are seventy or eighty yers of age [are driven] off in the cold to frieze and starve to death." The rebels, he said, were "doing all they can to prevent free labor, and reestablish a kind of secondary slavery."

The safety of the country "depenes upon giving the Colered man all the rights of a white man," said Holly. He asked the government official to help "pass some laws that will give protection to the colered men and meet out Justice to traters in arms."

Besides helping freedmen and women seek justice, black soldiers helped in organizing and building schools and churches for their communities. In the spring of 1866, members of the Third Colored Arkansas Volunteers built a home for orphaned children in Helena, Arkansas. "The Amount of work that has been done on the grounds by the Soldiers is immense," reported a company lieutenant. "From an allmost unbroken forest it has been cleared, fenced and a large part of it planted, and four substantial buildings erected suitable for the wants of the children and those who have the Care of them."

Former slaves regarded black soldiers as liberators and protectors. Former Confederates, on the other hand, saw them as living symbols of their defeat—of a world turned upside down. Wherever they looked, they saw black men in blue uniforms walking casually along city streets, carrying guns and acting for all the world as if they were equal, or even superior, to their former masters. For many people in the defeated South, the sight was unbearable.

Southern whites expressed their anger through taunts, threats, assaults, and even murder. Perhaps they hoped rough treatment would intimidate black soldiers and keep them from standing up for their rights. But they did not reckon with the effect military service had had on these men. Black veterans viewed themselves as citizens with rights; they had come too far to back down.

Threats and violence from the white community seemed only to intensify the commitment of black soldiers to help their people press for equality. Their resolve remained even after they left the military. Whether they returned to homes in the North or the South, thousands of black veterans continued to stand up for the rights they felt they had earned through their army service.

When the army failed to give them their back pay and bounties, the former soldiers persisted until the government paid up.

Many were owed several hundred dollars—a fortune to men who were hard-pressed and had counted on the money to settle their debts, buy a piece of land, and start a new life. Many black veterans hired "claim agents," often ex-army recruiters, to intervene with federal authorities. If that didn't work, they hired lawyers to pursue their claims.

In 1867, twenty-three former members of a black South Carolina regiment hired attorney E. G. Dudley to plead their case to the powerful anti-slavery senator from Massachusetts, Charles Sumner. Three years before, the veterans had bought homes sold at auction, paying one-fourth of the purchase price, with the understanding that they would pay the rest as soon as they received their government bounty and back pay. But the money never came, and the men faced losing their homes. Sumner was able to postpone the sale of the houses for a year to give the men a chance to obtain the money owed them.

Just as they refused to let the government cheat them, black veterans also refused to submit quietly to abuse by whites. Physical attacks against blacks who had served in the Union Army were common in the postwar South, especially in the border states. Former slaveowners felt betrayed by the Union, which had pledged not to interfere with slavery in their states as long as they remained loyal. What had their loyalty brought them but ruin? these men and women asked. Their slaves had run off, and their land lay idle for lack of workers to tend it. Who better to vent their rage on than these soldiers who had once been their slaves?

Instead of fighting back with their fists or guns, most black veterans sought justice from the local Freedmen's Bureau. The federal government established the bureau in early 1865 to feed, clothe, and house people left homeless by the war. But it was also responsible for settling disputes and protecting the legal rights of freed slaves.

After he was threatened and beaten by a white man named John Cornwell, black veteran James Cook went to the Freedmen's Bureau in his hometown of Brentsville, Virginia. Cook told the bureau agent that Cornwell had called him a "d——d black Yankee, son of a b——h," and shot at him. The bullet missed its mark, and Cook tried to run away, but Cornwell caught him, beat him with the butt of his gun, and dragged him to the local jail.

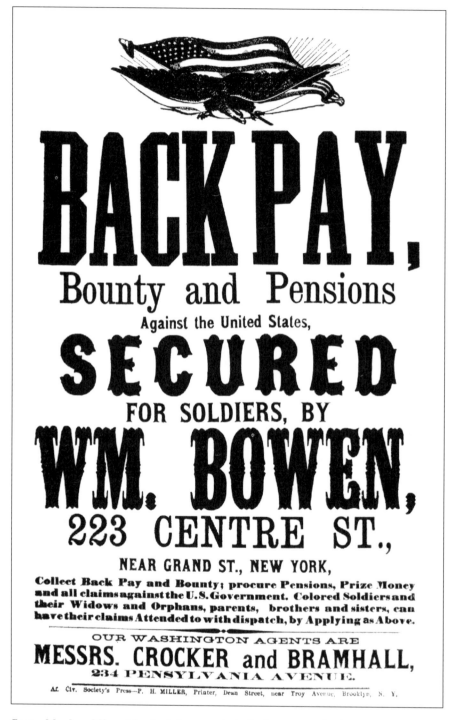

Some black soldiers hired claim agents to help secure the bounties and pensions owed them by the federal government. Agents earned a commission on every successful claim.

After hearing Cook's story, the Freedmen's Bureau agent called in Cornwell, who defended his actions by accusing the veteran of "impudence." This impudence, it turned out, consisted of Cook's telling the white man that he had been in the Union Army and was proud of it.

The local doctor, who had followed Cook to the bureau office, made it clear that the sympathies of the white community lay with Cornwell. "Subdued and miserable as we are," the doctor told the agent, "we will not allow niggers to come among us and brag about having been in the Yankee army. It is as much as we can do to tolerate it in white men."

In the victorious North, the sight of black men in army uniforms did not provoke the violent reaction it did in the South. Indeed, returning black veterans were often greeted by fanfare and cheering crowds. The town of Hartford, Connecticut, welcomed the men of the Twenty-ninth U.S. Colored Infantry with a brass band, speeches by local dignitaries, and a sumptuous meal prepared by the city's "white and colored citizens." But when the celebration was over, the veterans discovered that little had changed; the week before they came home the Hartford City Council had defeated a law that would have extended the right to vote to black citizens.

Civil War veterans led the fight to expand the rights of black Americans—the right to own property, to get an education, to earn a decent living, and to be treated as equals. In January 1867, twelve black Mississippi veterans wrote to their former commander to protest discriminatory treatment by local white officials. The local mayor had told black men that they could not rent a house or land, or even live in town, without a "white man to stand" for them. All black men had to have a contract proving that they were working for a white man.

The mayor's deputy was "taking people to jail all the time," wrote the veterans. Black men found traveling on the road were put in jail or forced to sign a contract and go to work as farm hands on a local plantation. "If this is the law of the United States we will submit," the ex-soldiers told their commander, "but if it is not we are willing to take our musket and surve three years longer [until we have] more liberty."

Determined to "labor for the development of his race," Sergeant

Elijah Marrs, the former slave from Kentucky who escaped to Union lines with twenty-seven other men, opened a school and later became a minister. Another black veteran, Henry Butler, fulfilled his dream of becoming "a teacher and assist my race to improve their station." Butler went through grade school, high school, and college,

After the War

After the homecoming parades and celebrations were over, black veterans had to find work. Sadly, their choices were often limited by discrimination and lack of experience. Most ended up in the same low-paying jobs they had held before the war, as day laborers in the North and field hands in the South. But many others obtained an education and trained for a profession or a skilled trade; others opened small businesses.

Private Junius B. Roberts managed to save four hundred dollars from his army wages and bounty. He used the money to pay for his education as a minister. An Ohio veteran used his savings to learn the bricklaying trade, which guaranteed good pay and plenty of work. By saving every dime he could, the former soldier was able to put all four of his children through college.

The dream of most southern black veterans was to own a piece of land on which they could farm. But land cost money—lots of money. One sergeant who served in the 128th U.S. Colored Infantry used his entire army savings of two hundred dollars to buy a small plot of land. When they could not afford to buy property of their own, some soldiers pooled their money and bought one large tract of land on which many families settled.

In the late 1870s, Thomas Wentworth Higginson, former commander of the First South Carolina Colored Volunteers, returned to South Carolina and Florida to revisit scenes of the war. He reported that in his travels he "rarely met an ex-soldier who did not own his house and ground . . . varying from five to two hundred acres."

Thousands of Civil War veterans wanted to stay in the army. They got their chance in July 1866, when Congress created six black regiments as part of the nation's regular army, two cavalry and four infantry (later reduced to two), all under white officers. Although the pay was low, it was equal to what white soldiers got, and it was steady; there was also less discrimination than in civilian life. Most of the 12,500 men who volunteered for these four regiments were Civil War veterans.

supporting himself with odd jobs. He got a degree in English and began a teaching career that spanned forty years.

Nowhere was the contribution of black veterans more important than in the struggle to secure the right to vote. "Without the rights of suffrage, we are without protection, and liable to . . . outrage,"

A few lucky veterans managed to buy small plots of land to call their own.

The two black infantry regiments, the Twenty-fourth and Twenty-fifth, manned forts along the U.S.-Mexican border and helped to quell violent land disputes between the two countries. The Ninth and Tenth cavalries spent most of their time in the West, where increased migration had sparked fighting between settlers and the Apaches, Sioux, Comanche, and other Native American tribes who were on the land first. Native Americans dubbed the black troops "Buffalo soldiers," because of their dark skin and the courage with which they fought.

argued a group of black veterans from Washington, D.C. They submitted a petition to Congress in December 1865, asking legislators to pass a law giving black men the right to vote. The petition was signed by 2,500 former soldiers. (Black men received voting rights in 1870 with ratification of the Fifteenth Amendment to the U.S. Constitution; women did not win the right to vote until 1920.)

Black veterans helped form local political organizations and played a major role in state and local freedmen's conventions held in 1865 and 1866. During Reconstruction—the twelve-year period following the Civil War when the South rebuilt its cities, economy, and political structure—at least forty-one black veterans served as delegates to state constitutional conventions. At the insistence of the federal government, the ex-Confederate states rewrote their constitutions, extending broader rights to black citizens, including the right to vote. Hundreds more veterans served in local and state offices under Reconstruction governments. Four black veterans from the South were elected to the U.S. Congress.

In the North, too, blacks who had served in the military worked as lobbyists and government officials, helping to shape the postwar policies that affected black Americans. Lewis Douglass of the Fifty-fourth Massachusetts joined a delegation that went to the White House to protest harsh new laws being imposed on freedmen and women in the South.

Many black veterans ran for political office following the Civil War. Here, a candidate delivers a speech to potential supporters.

Women, too, worked to improve the lives and expand the rights of black Americans. Harriet Tubman believed that real liberation could be achieved only by giving equal rights to black men and black women. In addition to her efforts on behalf of the poor, disabled, and elderly, she was active in many women's organizations.

Sojourner Truth, who worked with the Freedmen's Bureau and Freedmen's Relief Societies after the war, shared Tubman's dedication to equal rights for women. She fought throughout her life for women's suffrage.

For black, as for white, veterans, Civil War service was one of the most important times in their lives. To keep the experience alive, many formed and joined veterans organizations, including the Grand Army of the Republic, the oldest and largest such group in the country.

Ex-soldiers also got involved in veterans groups to make sure that America remembered their contributions and gave them the back pay and rights they had earned through army service. In 1867, a group of black veterans organized a "Convention of Colored Soldiers and Sailors" to press for black voting rights.

Sergeant William Carney, who had so bravely carried the flag for the Fifty-fourth Massachusetts during the assault on Fort Wagner, was among the speakers at a veterans' convention in Boston in 1887. Carney and other veterans called on the government to provide black citizens with "the full and equal protection of the laws."

The determination of black Americans to fight for their country and for freedom helped transform what began as a war to restore the Union into a struggle to end slavery.

Serving in the Union Army also transformed the lives of black soldiers. They had learned how to fight, not just against an armed enemy on the battlefield but also against less visible enemies such as injustice and racial discrimination. Soldiers took that knowledge home to their families and communities.

Black veterans did not return to a perfect world. Their shining performance in the army might have won them the respect of many whites, but it did not end racism or poverty, both of which continued to oppress black Americans.

Thanks to their military experience, thousands of black men understood for the first time what it meant to be a citizen of the United States. They understood the rights and responsibilities that went with citizenship. They also had the will to push for those rights—for themselves, their families, and their communities. It was a struggle that thousands of black veterans would remain committed to for the rest of their lives.

The Civil War veteran

Glossary

◆　◆　◆

abolitionist　a person who worked to end slavery in the United States

artillery　a branch of the armed forces that operates large mounted guns, too heavy to carry; also, the guns themselves

battery　a grouping of big guns, usually in several places along the wall of a fort or on a battlefield

bayonet　a long, narrow-bladed knife designed to fit on the end of a rifle barrel and to be used in hand-to-hand combat

border states　the four slave states—Maryland, Missouri, Kentucky, and Delaware—that remained in the Union during the Civil War and acted as a dividing line between the Union and the Confederacy

canister　small metal balls packed tightly with sawdust into a hollow metal case that scatter when shot out of a cannon

casualty　a soldier, who, during a battle, is wounded, killed, captured, or missing in action

cavalry　a branch of the army trained to fight on horseback

colors　a flag bearing the name and insignia of a particular military regiment

commissioned officer　any officer who holds a commission (a certificate giving military rank and authority) as a second lieutenant or above in the U.S. Army

Confederate States of America the alliance of eleven southern states that withdrew from the United States in 1860 and 1861: Alabama, Arkansas, Florida, Georgia, Louisiana, Mississippi, North Carolina, South Carolina, Tennessee, Texas, and Virginia

contraband a slave who escaped to or was brought into Union lines

earthwork a wall made of earth and used to protect soldiers and guns in the field or in a fort.

enlist to join the armed services

fatigue duty military labor performed by or assigned to soldiers

Federal having to do with the union of states that recognized the authority of the United States government based in Washington, D.C.

formation an arrangement or positioning of troops for battle or marching

fortification an earthen or stone wall, moat, piled tree branches, or other works built to defend or strengthen a position against the enemy

Freedmen's Bureau an agency established by the federal government early in 1865 to feed, clothe, and house people left homeless by the Civil War; also responsible for settling disputes and protecting the rights of freed slaves

grape shot a cluster of nine solid iron balls stacked in three levels, held together by metal plates and a nut and bolt, and fired out of a cannon

infantry a branch of the army made up of units trained to fight on foot

latrine an outdoor toilet

musket a long-barreled gun carried by infantry and fired from the shoulder

muster to call together a group of soldiers; to enlist someone in, or discharge someone from, military service

parapet a wall of earth or stone built along the edge of a fort to protect soldiers and their big guns from enemy attack

picket one or more soldiers who stand guard outside a camp or fort to warn of enemy approach

plantation a large estate or farm where crops are planted and harvested

rebel　another term for Confederate soldier

recruit　to persuade a person to join the armed services; a person who enlists in the armed services

regiment　a military unit. In Civil War times, a regiment consisted of between seven hundred and one thousand soldiers, typically from the same state.

shell　a hollow metal case containing an explosive bursting charge; used to fire canister and other weapons out of artillery during the Civil War

Union　another name for the United States of America, used especially during the Civil War

U.S. Bureau of Colored Troops　established by the Union government to create, find officers for, and oversee black regiments during the Civil War

veteran　a former member of the armed services

Yankee　another name for Northerner

Selected Bibliography

◆　◆　◆

More than fifty thousand books have been written about the Civil War. Research for this publication alone involved several hundred sources, including books, diaries, letters, newspapers, and other documents. What follows is a short list of books and newspapers offering further information about black soldiers in the Civil War.

Berlin, Ira, et al., eds. *The Destruction of Slavery. (Freedom: A Documentary History of Emancipation, 1861–1867, Vol. 1, no. 1).* New York: Cambridge University Press, 1985.

———. *The Black Military Experience. (Freedom: A Documentary History of Emancipation, 1861–1867, no. 2).* New York: Cambridge University Press, 1982.

———. *Free at Last: A Documentary History of Slavery, Freedom, and the Civil War.* New York: The New Press, 1992.

Bradford, Sarah H. *Harriet Tubman: The Moses of Her People.* New York: J. J. Little & co., 1901. Reprint. New York: Corinth Books, 1961.

Brown, William Wells. *The Negro in the American Rebellion.* Boston: Lee & Shepard, 1867. Reprint. New York: The Citadel Press, 1971.

Clark, Peter H. *The Black Brigade of Cincinnati.* New York: Arno Press, 1969.

Cornish, Dudley Taylor. *The Sable Arm: Black Troops in the Union Army, 1861–1865.* New York: Longmans, Green, 1956. Reprint. Lawrence, Kansas: University Press of Kansas, 1987.

Douglass, Frederick. *Life and Times of Frederick Douglass.* New York: Collier Books, 1962.

Franklin, John Hope. *From Slavery to Freedom.* 5th ed. New York: Knopf, 1980.

Glatthaar, Joseph T. *Forged in Battle: The Civil War Alliance of Black Soldiers and White Soldiers.* New York: Meridian, 1991.

Gooding, Corporal James Henry. *On the Altar of Freedom: A Black Soldier's Civil War Letters from the Front.* Edited by Virginia A. Adams. New York: Warner Books, 1991.

Hallowell, Norwood P. *The Negro as a Soldier in the War of the Rebellion.* Boston: Little, Brown and Company, 1897.

Higginson, Thomas Wentworth. *Army Life in a Black Regiment*. Boston: Fields, Osgood & Company, 1870. Reprint. New York: Collier Books, 1962.

Litwack, Leon F. *Been in the Storm So Long: The Aftermath of Slavery*. New York: Vintage, 1980.

Main, Edwin M. *The Story of the Marches, Battles and Incidents of the Third United States Colored Calvary*. Globe Printing Company, 1908. Reprint. New York: Negro Universities Press, 1970.

Marrs, Elijah P. *Life and History of the Rev. Elijah P. Marrs*. Louisville, Kentucky: The Bradley & Gilbert Company, 1885. Reprint. Miami: Mnemosyne Publishing Company, 1969.

McPherson, James M. *Marching Toward Freedom: The Negro in the Civil War, 1861–1865*. New York: Facts on File, 1991.

———. *Struggle for Equality: Abolitionists and the Negro in the Civil War and Reconstruction*. Princeton, N.J.: Princeton University Press, 1964.

———. *The Negro's Civil War: How American Blacks Felt and Acted During the War for the Union*. New York: Ballantine Books, 1991.

Mellon James, ed. *Bullwhip Days, The Slaves Remember: An Oral History*. New York: Weidenfeld & Nicholson, 1988.

Meltzer, Milton, ed. *The Black Americans: A History in Their Own Words, 1619–1865*. New York: Thomas Y. Crowell Company, 1964. Reprint. New York: Harper Trophy, 1987.

Quarles, Benjamin. *The Negro in the Civil War*. New York: De Capo Press, 1953.

Rawick, George P., ed. *The American Slave: A Composite Autobiography*. 19 vols. Westport, Conn.: Greenwood Press, 1972.

Redky, Edwin S., ed. *A Grand Army of Black Men: Letters from African-American Soldiers in the Union Army, 1861–1865*. New York: Cambridge University Press, 1992.

Rose, Willie Lee. *Rehearsal for Reconstruction: The Port Royal Experiment*. New York: Oxford University Press, 1964.

Sterling, Dorothy. *Captain of the Planter: The Story of Robert Smalls*. Garden City, N.Y.: Doubleday, 1958.

Taylor, Susie King. *A Black Woman's Civil War Memoirs: Reminiscences of My Life in Camp*. Boston: Susie King Taylor, 1902. Reprint. New York: Arno Press and The New York Times, 1968.

Wesley, Charles H. and Patricia W. Romero. *Negro Americans in the Civil War: From Slavery to Citizenship*. 2d ed. New York: Publishers Company, 1969.

Williams, George W. *A History of the Negro Troops in the War of the Rebellion, 1861–1865*. New York: Harper & Brothers, 1888. Reprint. New York: Negro Universities Press, 1969.

Wilson, Joseph T. *The Black Phalanx*. Hartford, Conn.: American Publishing Co., 1892. Reprint. New York: Arno Press and The New York Times, 1968.

Black-owned Newspapers

The Anglo-African, New York, 1859–1865.

Christian Recorder, newspaper of the African Methodist Episcopal Church, Philadelphia, 1852–1960.

Douglass' Monthly, edited and published by Frederick Douglass in Rochester, New York, 1858–1863.

Acknowledgments

◆　　◆　　◆

I am especially grateful to Steven F. Miller of the Freedmen and Southern Society Project at the University of Maryland, whose editorial guidance and support were invaluable. I also want to thank Joseph P. Reidy in the Department of History at Howard University and Jenice View of the Union Institute in Washington, D.C., for their insightful reading of the manuscript and advice on how to improve it. Thanks also to Pamela Wilson and Peggy Denker, who stuck with me through endless drafts and questions, and to Chris Laing and Norm Bolotin of Laing Communications for giving me the opportunity to write for children.

For help in tracking down hard-to-find images and information, I am grateful to the staff at the Library of Congress; the Schomburg Center for Research in Black Culture, New York; Leib Image Archives, York, Pennsylvania; the Moorland-Spingarn Research Center at Howard University; the U.S. Army Military History Institute, Carlisle, Pennsylvania; and the Chicago Historical Society. Thanks also to Jim Enos, retired colonel, U.S. Air Force.

Finally, thanks to all the people, young and not so young, who read the manuscript in draft: Nico Matsakis, Nina Robbins, Iris Rothman, Terry Coye, Glee Murray, Michelle Lamboy, Maya Prabhu, Elana and Janna Berger, Vicky Ward, Sarah Hale, Andy Dickenson, and Cory O'Brien.

Index

Page numbers in *italics* refer to photographs and illustrations.

Picture Credits

◆　　◆　　◆

The photographs and illustrations in this book are from the following sources. The images are public domain or are used with the source's permission.

Association for the Study of Black Life and History, Washington, D.C. • pages x, 27, 76, 101

The Black Phalanx (American Publishing Co., Hartford, Conn., 1892) • pages 2, 55, 56, 70, 71

Chicago Historical Society • page 45

Fort Sumter National Monument, Sullivan's Island, S.C. • page vi

Freedmen and Southern Society Project, College Park, Md. • pages 13, 14, 42, 48, 78, 80–81, 85, 90, 95

Harper's Weekly • (March 14, 1863) page 36, (May 4, 1867) page 105

Leib Image Archives, York, Pa. • pages ii, 4, 5, 12, 34–35, 46, 51, 58, 87

Library of Congress, Washington, D.C. • pages 6–7, 9, 11, 16–17, 41, 50, 66–67, 68, 72, 75, 86, 92–93, 102–103

Moorland-Spingarn Research Center, Howard University, Washington, D.C. • pages 31, 33

National Archives, Washington, D.C. • pages 25, 29, 38–39, 83, 84

New York Public Library • page 19

Schomburg Center for Research in Black Culture, The New York Public Library • pages 22, 30, 44, 62

U.S. Army Military History Institute, Carlisle Barracks, Pa. • pages 8, 20, 52–53